The
LASTING
IMPACT *of*
POSITIVE
LEADERSHIP

STAN TOLER

Cover design by Kyler Dougherty

The Lasting Impact of Positive Leadership
Copyright © 2019 by Stan Toler
Published by Harvest House Publishers
Eugene, Oregon 97408
www.harvesthousepublishers.com

ISBN 978-0-7369-7498-1 (pbk)
ISBN 978-0-7369-7499-8 (eBook)

Library of Congress Cataloging-in-Publication Data is on file at the Library of Congress, Washington, DC

Printed in the United States of America
19 20 21 22 23 24 25 26 27 / VP-GL / 10 9 8 7 6 5 4 3 2 1

Contents

Foreword by John C. Maxwell

Positive leadership that provides a lasting impact"—that phrase describes what leaders strive to achieve. It raises the bar for leaders who want to pursue this level of excellence. And it defines a leader not based on a position, but the person.

When I think about positive leadership, Stan Toler is one of the few people that I place in this category. How do I know this? I have known Stan for nearly my entire life. We were boyhood friends. My dad, Dr. Melvin Maxwell, was his college president and encouraged him to follow his call to the ministry. Anyone mentored under my dad's ministry was one of his boys for life.

Stan and I attended college together. When I started out in the ministry as pastor of a church in Ohio, the first staff member I hired was Stan. That began a fruitful professional association. Through the years we have had countless opportunities to work together. But there's another reason I'm highly biased about the person who Stan is and how great this book is.

For years, I've talked and written on leadership. Most people never get past the point of talking about it. I promise you, it's much easier to "talk the talk" than to "walk the talk." There are only a few who execute the role of being an exceptional leader—the subject of another book that Stan has masterfully written. The premise that Stan writes of in *The Lasting Impact of Positive Leadership* is one that relates to and motivates leaders through practical principles.

Readers, once you start this book, don't expect to put it down until the end. While most leadership books are more business-related, *The Lasting Impact of Positive Leadership* focuses on the practical principles and embracing the essential qualities of being, first, a leader as a person who sets the foundation in his or her own life, then having a lasting impact on others.

If you follow the simple yet profound wisdom in this book, then you, too, will take leadership to a level that you've never experienced. Enjoy!

—John C. Maxwell
Founder and CEO of the John Maxwell Company
a #1 *New York Times* bestselling author, speaker, and coach
with more than 30 million units sold in 50 languages

What Does Your Leadership Reveal About You?

If you believe you can, you probably can. If you believe you won't, you most assuredly won't. Belief is the ignition switch that gets you off the launching pad.

—Denis Waitley

Whether you're in the ministry business, politics, education, or community service, people are talking not only about the need for more leaders but also the need for better leaders. The rapid rate of change at the dawn of the twenty-first century has created a need for those who will lead at a higher dimension. Mere mental or physical manipulation doesn't cut it anymore; organizations and societies have evolved beyond traditional modes of influence. People want more. Effective leaders today draw from creating a synergy for change and organizational vitality. Throughout history many great leaders have led this way with their heads, hearts, and souls. This kind of leading is not optional if the end goal is effective leadership.

Many are intimidated by the gleaming, breathing leadership icons. Yet the principles by which they lead are within the grasp of most of us.

Where are you as a leader? What defines you as a leader? Is it more about your performance versus your attitude? Is it more focused on self-leadership versus servant leadership? How do others perceive you? Are you modeling godly leadership or leadership dictated by "the pressure of achieving successful results"?

These questions (and many others) are not always simple to answer. In fact, the end result is far beyond defining just one answer. Rather it's a process based on how a leader responds over time that reveals the leader's true identity. And often, the simple formula for a leader's success starts and ends with a positive outlook.

"But whoever desires
to become great
among you, let him
be your servant. And
whoever desires to be
first among you, let
him be your slave."

Matthew 20:26-27 (NKJV)

Chapter 1

The Power of a Positive Mind

Great minds have purposes, others have wishes.

—WASHINGTON IRVING

For centuries medical professionals have studied the human condition through the lens of disease. That means they have generally paid less attention to healthy people than to the sick, and they have focused their attention on what's wrong with the goal of making it better. They've focused on the symptoms and root causes of illness and tried to alleviate or eliminate them. That has been true also in the relatively new medical specialty of psychology. It has been driven largely by the attempt to identify and eliminate mental illness.

However, there is an emerging focus on wellness in the practice of medicine, and that exists within the practice of psychology as well. *Positive psychology* focuses on fostering positive attitudes toward one's experiences, individual traits, and life events with the goal of minimizing destructive thoughts and creating a sense of optimism toward life. Positive psychology examines how ordinary people can become happier and more fulfilled.

Barbara L. Fredrickson, a researcher at the University of Michigan, found that positive thinking is more than just a feel-good exercise; it actually changes the way your brain works. In her experiment, Fredrickson divided her subjects into five groups and showed each group different video clips, each intended to foster a different kind of emotional response. The first group saw clips intended to create feelings of joy, the second group feelings of hope, the fourth group feelings of fear, and the fifth group feelings of anger. The third group was the control group, so they watched videos that did not evoke any emotional response.

Afterward, Fredrickson asked each person to imagine themselves in a situation where they would experience similar emotions to what they had just seen and write down what they would do in response. Each person had a piece of paper with twenty blank lines that began with the words, "I would like to…"

Here's where it gets interesting. People who saw images that evoked fear or anger wrote down the fewest responses, but those who saw images of joy and contentment recorded many more. Fredrickson concluded that when we experience positive emotions such as love, joy, and contentment, we see more possibilities for our lives. Positive emotions actually make us think bigger while negative emotions limit our sense of possibility. Frederickson wrote that "positive emotions broaden an individual's momentary thought-action repertoire: joy sparks the urge to play, interest sparks the urge to explore, contentment sparks the urge to savor and integrate, and love sparks a recurring cycle of each of these urges within safe, close relationships. The broadened mindsets arising from these positive emotions are contrasted to the narrowed mindsets sparked by many negative emotions (i.e. specific action tendencies, such as attack or flee)."[1]

This means that when you dwell on negative thoughts such as complaining, worry, anger, anxiety, and forgiveness, it shuts down your brain's ability to cope with problems and find solutions. But when you entertain thoughts of hope, love, and joy, you increase your mind's ability to solve problems and create a better future. Positive thinking actually changes your brain.

There's more. Fredrickson also wrote, "Positive emotions promote discovery of novel and creative actions, ideas and social bonds, which in turn build that individual's personal resources…that can be drawn on later to improve the odds of successful coping and survival."[2] Positive thoughts lead to increased "social bonds," which become a resource for the future. That's a complex way of saying that positive thinking increases your influence with others.

Fredrickson summarized her findings this way:

> When positive emotions are in short supply, people get stuck. They lose their degrees of behavioral freedom and become painfully predictable. But when positive emotions are in ample supply, people take off. They become generative, creative, resilient, ripe with possibility and beautifully complex. The broaden-and-build theory conveys how positive emotions move people forward and lift them to the higher ground of optimal well-being.[3]

While it may have taken a psychological study for many to accept these ideas, they have been obvious to positive thinkers for centuries. Positive thinking results in a greater sense of personal well-being—plus it increases your ability to solve problems, make friends, and influence others. The key to broadening your influence is something you already have: your mind. All you have to do is activate it with positive thoughts.

A Positive Attitude Creates Possibility

Roger Crawford makes his living as a consultant and public speaker. He's written books and travels all the across the country working with Fortune 500 companies, national and state associations, and school districts. Those aren't bad credentials. But if that doesn't impress you, how about this: Before becoming a consultant, he was a varsity tennis player for Loyola Marymount University and later became a professional tennis player certified by the United States Tennis Association. Still not impressed? Would you change your opinion if I told you Roger has no hands and only one foot?

Roger Crawford was born with a condition called *ectrodactylism*. When he emerged from his mother's womb, the doctors saw that he had a thumb-like projection extending out of his right forearm and a thumb and finger growing out of his left forearm. He had no palms. His legs and arms were shortened. And his left leg possessed a shrunken foot with only three toes. At age five, Roger's foot was amputated. His parents were told by various medical professionals that he would never be able to walk, probably would not be able to take care of himself, and would never lead a normal life.

After recovering from the shock, Roger's parents were determined to give him the best chance possible for living a normal life.

They raised him to feel loved, to be strong, and to develop independence. "You're only as handicapped as you want to be," his father used to tell him. They encouraged him to do everything his heart desired. And they taught him to think positively.

Roger appreciated the encouragement and training he received from his parents, but I don't think he really understood the significance of it or his achievements until he was in college and interacted with someone who wanted to meet him. After receiving a phone call from a man who had read about his tennis victories, Crawford agreed to meet him at a nearby restaurant. When Roger stood up to shake hands with the man, he discovered that the other guy had hands that were almost identical to his. That not only caught his attention but got him excited because he thought he had found someone similar to him but older who could act as his mentor.

However, after talking with the stranger for a few minutes, Roger discovered that this man was bitter and pessimistic and blamed all of life's disappointments and failures on his disabilities. He had never held a job long, and he was sure this was because of "discrimination." But as he continued sharing, it was clearly not the reason. As the man admitted, he was constantly late, frequently absent, and failed to take responsibility for his work. His attitude was "The world owes me," and his problem was that the world disagreed. He was even angry with Roger because he didn't share his despair.

Roger and the man kept in touch for several years, until it dawned on Roger that even if some miracle were suddenly to give this man a perfect body, his unhappiness and lack of success wouldn't change. He would still be in the same place in his life. Obviously, the man had allowed failure to seize him from the inside.

Chances are that the adversity in your life has been nowhere near as difficult as Roger Crawford's. And that's why his story is such an inspiration. Roger maintained that handicaps can only disable those that let them. This is true not only of physical challenges but of emotional and intellectual ones as well. Limitations only become real and lasting when they are created in our minds, not from our bodies.

Attitudes determine actions. What you think you are, you are. We are either the masters or the victims of our attitudes. It's a matter of personal choice—blessing or curse.

The Right Attitude Comes First

Attitude makes all the difference. The development of a positive attitude is the first conscious step toward becoming an effective leader. Successful leadership cannot be constructed without this crucial building block. Check out the following attitude axioms suggested by the words and actions of Joshua and Caleb in the Bible:

- Our attitude determines our approach to life.
- Our attitude determines our relationship with people.
- Our attitude is often the only difference between success and failure.
- Our attitude at the beginning of a task will affect its outcomes more than anything else.
- Our attitude can turn problems into blessings.
- Our attitude is not automatically good just because we belong to God.

A change of attitude is like changing your mind. You just decide you are going to change the way you see things. You can't just pretend you have a good attitude. You have to have a good attitude.

You have to continually look at the bright side of situations, the good side of people—including yourself—and the positive side of negative events.

Positive Thinkers Get Positive Results

The minute you mention the word *problem*, the implication is that you are speaking negatively. But some don't see it that way.

People often asked Norman Vincent Peale, "Don't you think life would be better if we had few problems?" Norman would answer that question by saying, "I'll be happy to take you to Woodlawn Cemetery because the only people I know who don't have any problems are dead."

Norman thought it was possible that the more problems you have, the more alive you are. "If you have no problems at all," he would say, "you're in grave jeopardy!" In fact, if you really insisted that you had no problems, he would suggest that you immediately race home, go straight to your bedroom, and get down on your knees and pray, "What's the matter, Lord? Don't you trust me anymore? Give me some problems!"

The Power of Positive Influences

Surround yourself with positive influences. When you are surrounded by negative thinkers, images, or materials, it is easy to get bogged down in hopelessness.

Read inspiring books and magazines. Listen to motivational recordings and speakers. Attend positive-thinking seminars or programs. Make it a point to read or watch or listen to something positive or inspiring at least once every day.

Associate with positive people. Look for friends who feel good about themselves, people who have the attitude of gratitude. People who need to tear down others are not happy with themselves and are not good for you or your attitude.

The Power of a Positive Attitude

Norman Cousins had problems, primarily health related, that affected him for much of his life. A journalist and editor, he began his career as a book critic for a magazine and soon became managing editor. In 1940, he joined *Saturday Review of Literature,* and two years later was named editor-in-chief. During his thirty years in that position, circulation increased from 20,000 to an astounding 650,000. At one time, Cousins became seriously ill and was diagnosed with a degenerative inflammatory disease, which caused him considerable pain. He also suffered from heart disease, and doctors gave him little chance of survival. But Cousins was a firm believer in the power of a positive attitude, and he refused to accept the prognosis he'd received. "Optimism doesn't wait on facts," he said, "it deals with prospects. Pessimism is a waste of time."

Cousins checked himself out of the hospital and into a nearby hotel, where he self-prescribed megadoses of vitamin C combined with laughter. He began watching classic Marx Brothers films over and over. The result? Cousins made the joyous discovery that ten minutes of genuine belly laughter had an anesthetic effect and would give him at least two hours of pain-free sleep. Short-term relief is one thing, but did Cousins's positive mental attitude have any long-range benefits? Considering the fact that he lived for sixteen productive and successful years beyond what his doctors predicted, the answer is clearly yes!

Taking the positive view requires more than simply casting out negative thoughts—although that is an important part of it. Positive input must replace negative thoughts. The quickest way to cast out negative thoughts is to feed enough positive thoughts into your mind that there is no longer room for the negative thoughts.

People who take the positive view basically see the world as a good place. They actively look for the good in other people and situations, and they act with hope and faith.

W. Clement Stone was a successful businessman, author, and philanthropist. A strong proponent of the power of attitude, he first gained fame in 1960 as the coauthor, with Napoleon Hill, of *Success Through a Positive Mental Attitude*. During a lifetime that spanned a century, he continued to champion the philosophy that the right attitude could overcome virtually every problem: "So you've got a problem? That's good! Why? Because repeated victories over your problems are the rungs on your ladder to success. With each victory you grow in wisdom, stature, and experience. You become a bigger, better, more successful person each time you meet a problem and tackle and conquer it with a positive mental attitude."[4]

Help Others Feel Good About Themselves

People who have positive self-esteem tend to be genuinely helpful to other people. In fact, the two tendencies go together so well that it is hard to tell which produces the other. It's probably a little bit of both. Those who feel good about themselves long to help others feel good about themselves. The more they reach out to help others, the better they feel about themselves. Only the insecure, the frightened, the people with low self-esteem approach life with an attitude that says, "It's every person for himself or herself." Sadly, they find only more insecurity and lower self-esteem.

Mother Teresa stated it best, "Let no one ever come to you without leaving better and happier."

Positive Habits Predict Success

In 1989, Stephen R. Covey published the bestselling book *The 7 Habits of Highly Effective People.* Covey may have been the first person to point out the link between our outlook and the habits they engender, habits that can set us up for success. These habits require little explanation. Notice how many of them are the opposite of the poor habits noted above.[5]

1. Be proactive.
2. Begin with the end in mind.
3. Put first things first.
4. Think win-win.
5. Seek first to understand, then to be understood.
6. Synergize (work together).
7. Sharpen the saw (replenish yourself).

What a different picture these habits draw than the negative habits we've discussed. Imagine the people who live this way. They have a positive idea of what they'd like to accomplish, and they take action on it. They don't procrastinate but have a bias for taking action. Far from being fearful of people and opportunities, they have an abundance mindset and gladly share with others, listen to others, and work together. Finally, they take care of themselves because they realize that their own well-being is their best resource.

Notice, too, that each of these habits stems from a positive outlook. To begin behaving in these ways by habit—that is, without thinking further about them—you must believe something positive about yourself, about others, and about the world. Positive habits set you up to achieve. They're the best predictor of your future success and happiness.

Covey's seven habits are well known, but there are many other positive habits that stem from a positive outlook. If you think positively, you'll almost certainly develop some of these good habits, which will in turn put you on a course for a better future.

It's all about creating the right habits. Good habits (or best practices) are hard to develop but they are easy to live with. Bad habits are easy to develop but they are hard to live with. In the end, develop good habits.

Chapter 2

The Power of Optimism

*I can't change the direction of the wind, but I can
adjust my sails to reach my destination.*

—JIMMY DEAN

O*ptimism* is often used as a catchall term for positive thinking,
but let's think about what the word really means. The term
can be traced to the philosopher Gottfried Wilhelm Leibniz, who
concluded that the world in which we live is the "best (optimum)
among all possible worlds."[1] In the best possible world, the best possible circumstances must exist and everything must be getting better rather than worse. So, classic optimism is usually seen as a naïve,
unrealistic notion about the goodness of the world and the virtuous
nature of human beings. But it's not at all what we mean by optimism as a form of positive thinking.

You're not what you
think you are. What
you think, you are.

–Unknown

Of course, we know that evil exists in the world, so optimism is not a simplistic belief that all of life's circumstances are somehow good. Neither does optimism require a belief that the world is always getting better. We know from history that great evils have been perpetrated again and again in the form of war, disease, and natural disaster. What we mean by optimism is the hopeful thought that better possibilities do exist and that they are in fact *more likely* to occur than negative ones. The optimist believes that, all things being equal, it'll probably all work out for the best. And usually it does.

For example, when the stock market takes a downturn, as it often does, one risk is that it will lead to a great crash, producing a worldwide economic depression in which millions are unemployed and people are left homeless and begging for food. That could happen. But an optimist knows that it probably won't and doesn't spend time worrying about it. She believes that, while things may be more difficult for a time, she probably won't lose her job or her house, and things will work out fine in the end. An optimist knows that when he is delayed by an accident on the freeway, it's possible that he'll miss the sales opportunity—but that's unlikely. More likely is that the client will understand that traffic can be unpredictable and offer another chance to make the pitch. Optimists think about what's most likely to happen rather than focusing on the less likely—and more frightful—things that probably won't come to pass. Therefore, optimists seldom waste brainpower on anxiety, worry, or gloomy thoughts about the future. That frees their minds to engage in creative possibilities and problem solving.

Optimists are more likely to influence others because it is a form of thought leadership. People are naturally drawn to positive thoughts and wish to avoid negative ones—even if they may be thinking them. As you give voice to the real probability that there are better days ahead, despite the current circumstances, others will listen to you. Remember, optimism does not mean dismissing problems or being unwilling to face challenges squarely. This is not a form of denial. It's a determination to focus on the best outcomes, and then work to make them reality.

If you want to influence others, practice optimistic thinking. Don't allow your mind to dwell on frightening but remote possibilities. Spend your brainpower on the more likely, more positive outcomes of a situation. That positive thinking will draw others to you.

Watch What You Think

Did you know that what you think powerfully impacts who you are? What you think about yourself, what you think about the world, what you think about others, what you think about your prospects in life—everything you think has an impact on the kind of person you are and will become.

Conduct a little research of your own. For the next week, pay special attention to how people answer the question "How are you?" That question gets asked and answered millions of times each day. You probably answer it yourself more than once every day. It's interesting to listen to the answers people give to describe how they're doing:

"Not bad."

"So-so, I guess."

"Pretty good."

"Fantastic!"

"Terrible!"

"So far, so good!"

"Not bad under the circumstances."

For every strong, positive, optimistic answer you hear from people, you'll probably hear eight or ten that range from neutral to pessimistic. If people really are doing as poorly as I hear them say they're doing, I'm not sure why they get out of bed!

Over the years, I've been answering the "How are you?" question with something like, "Why, I'm doing better than good!" I answer that way because I truly expect things to be and become better than good. Bestselling author, financial advisor, and radio host Dave Ramsey consistently answers, "Better than I deserve," and this has become one of his signature trademarks.

Why answer positively? I have learned through the years that for reasons I can't scientifically or even theologically explain, how I expect things to be greatly influences how they become. "Better than good" is such an optimistic approach to life, and there's a much greater chance that you will be remembered when you respond positively instead of neutrally or negatively. Plus, it will catch on! Nothing is as infectious as optimism and a positive outlook.

Sometimes, all it takes is a word, a phrase, or a thought planted in someone's mind to change his or her whole life. It truly pays to watch closely what and how you think. Frank Outlaw is said to have expressed the power of our thoughts this way:

> Watch your thoughts; they become words.
>
> Watch your words; they become actions.
>
> Watch your actions; they become habits.
>
> Watch your habits; they become character.
>
> Watch your character, for it becomes your destiny.

Lead good people
down a wrong path
and you'll come to
a bad end;
do good and you'll be
rewarded for it.

Proverbs 28:10 (MSG)

Optimist or Pessimist? It's Your Choice

Whether you are an optimist or a pessimist, the choice as to how you will be in the future is yours and yours alone. If you are like the people who aren't happy unless they are miserable, you can stay that way. If you want to be joyful, enthusiastic, and excited about life, you can be, regardless of your circumstances.

Optimistic, positive people spring out of bed in the morning and say, "Good morning, Lord!" Pessimistic, negative people pull the covers over their heads and moan, "Good Lord, it's morning again!"

Success is mainly a question of attitude. If you go into an under-taking expecting to succeed, the odds are great that you will succeed. If you go in fearing you'll lose, you're more likely to lose.

If two evenly matched football teams clash on the field, which one is likely to win? In all likelihood, the school with a winning tra-dition will pull out the victory. That's because its players expect to win. If a team has a losing tradition, its players are often surprised by a victory, which is why they have a mediocre season even when they're loaded with talent.

It's been said that the late Paul "Bear" Bryant, legendary foot-ball coach at the University of Alabama, went into each game with a winning attitude that was worth at least one touchdown for the Crimson Tide.

Winners are proactive not reactive. They create new circum-stances, not simply respond to circumstances. Reactive people are likely to go through life complaining about their circumstances. They focus on things they can do nothing about and ignore the things that are within their circle of influence. Proactive people look for ways to succeed in spite of any circumstances.

If you live in a northern state, you can stay inside during the winter and complain about the snow and the cold conditions. Or you can determine what winter activities you enjoy and get outside and do them. If you live in a large city, you can complain about traffic congestion and the cost of parking, or you can carpool or use public transportation. If you're a high school graduate, you can complain about the scarcity of jobs for people without college or technical training, or you can go and pursue additional education or training.

The pessimist screens out all the exciting promises that a moment can bring, while the optimist is ready and eager for each and every moment no matter the potential for a promise. Pessimists are either longing for a better moment, which may someday come, or reliving a more pleasant moment that is passed. But optimists are willing to trust in their plans for the future and in their ability to carry them out. They are willing to savor the memories of the past. Most of all, they are alert to the opportunities that each moment has to give.

Your future is the place to build momentum. You can take charge of your life without awareness of where you've been, where you are, and where you are going. But you can't build your life on the past. The past is gone. Nor can you allow your destiny to be limited by present circumstances. The present is fleeting. The only place left to build your life is in the future.

You can let the future happen, or you can create it. You create by forming a clear, vivid picture of what you want and by fixing your mental and emotional eyes on that picture. Let it become your vision, and it will draw you toward fulfillment.

Self-confidence is often little more than a feeling, way down in the pit of your stomach, that you can do something that seems impossible. But as you respond positively to that little feeling, it grows and grows until it reaches full bloom in concrete action. Sustainable confidence comes from competence and leads to commitment.

People who have strong self-confidence tend to apply their personal power to useful goals. They let others talk about their abilities and deeds. They concentrate on goals, not activities. And they freely express admiration and appreciation to others. It is enough for them to know the value of their goals and to believe in their abilities to reach those goals. They are far more concerned that their actions speak louder than their words.

Your life is as precious to you as the greatest people's lives have been to them. And your estimate of your self-worth is the only estimate that counts. What other people think about you is your reputation. What God knows about you is your character. What you think about yourself represents your true worth. Thomas Edison's teachers thought he was just another hard-of-hearing, slow-witted kid. Edison knew better and he showed them.

You have abundant potential. All you need to do is to convince yourself that the potential is there. And then execute with faith and with courage.

Winners are part of all humankind. Some see themselves as doing a job. Winners see themselves as a part of all humankind and their work as their contribution to a better world. George Bernard Shaw, the great English playwright, put it this way:

> I am convinced that my life belongs to the whole community and as long as I live, it is my privilege to do for it whatever I can, for the harder I work the more I live.

I will instruct you
and teach you
in the way you
should go;
I will counsel
you with my
loving eye on you.

Psalm 32:8

I rejoice in life for its own sake. Life is no brief candle for me. It is a sort of splendid torch which I have got hold of for a moment, and I want to make it burn as brightly as I possibly can before turning it over to future generations. [2]

Winners are proactive. Cultivate a winning attitude. It will sustain you even when the odds seem stacked against you.

You can live every day of your life and it may not feel as though you're achieving everything you want or need to. The law of inertia holds that a body at rest tends to remain at rest, and a body in motion tends to remain in motion, at the same speed and in the same direction, unless acted upon by an outside force. With one major difference, that law applies very well to the pattern of our lives.

People who are successful tend to remain successful.

People who are happy tend to remain happy.

People who are respected tend to remain respected.

People who reach their goals tend to go on reaching their goals.

So what's the major difference? In physics, inertia is controlled by outside forces; but the real changes in the directions of our lives come from inside us. As William James said, "The greatest discovery of my generation is that a person can alter his life by altering his attitude of mind."

You can live every day of your life. You can accomplish virtually any worthwhile goal you set for yourself. With an optimistic outlook and a positive attitude, you can achieve what you set out to accomplish.

Possibility

The late pastor and author Robert Schuller coined the term *possibility thinking* to describe another aspect of positive thought. In contrast to those who see only negative outcomes—the "glass half empty" thinkers—Schuller wrote: "The possibility thinkers perceptively probe every problem, proposal, and opportunity to discover the positive aspects present in almost every human situation. They are people—just like you—who when faced with a mountain do not quit. They keep on striving until they climb over, find a pass through, tunnel underneath—or simply stay and turn their mountain into a gold mine."[3]

Possibility thinking looks at every situation with this question in mind: "What good can we find in this?" Possibility thinking is exemplified in the line from George Bernard Shaw, famously quoted by Robert F. Kennedy, "Some people see things as they are and say why? I dream things that never were and say, why not?"[4] Possibility thinkers are convinced that a good outcome is possible no matter how difficult the situation may be. This goes beyond optimism, the idea that the worst possible result is unlikely, to probe for a positive outcome when disaster seems certain.

I love this story, embellished no doubt, about two boys who were twins, one a natural possibility thinker and the other a die-hard pessimist. The boys' parents noticed the difference in their temperaments and took them to a psychologist for evaluation. The doctor observed them and concluded that he could change their outlook and, therefore, their behavior.

The psychologist placed the pessimistic child in a room filled with all the toys any boy could want. He put the possibility thinker in a room filled with horse manure. "That should adjust their attitudes," he stated confidently. A video camera placed in each room allowed the doctor and parents to observe both children.

Contrary to all expectations, the pessimistic child continued to have a dour attitude, complaining that he had nobody to play with. Surrounded by all the good things in life, he continued to see the world in a negative light. Then the psychologist and parents looked in on the other child. They were amazed to find him digging through the manure. The psychologist ran into the room and asked what on earth the boy was doing. He said, "With all this manure, there's got to be a pony in there somewhere!"

Possibility thinkers are always influencers because people are always looking for fresh possibilities. Even negative thinkers long for a better world. They're just convinced no positive change is possible. If you can show others realistic prospects they have not yet seen, even confirmed pessimists will rally to your side. Everyone wants to believe in possibilities. Some are simply too tired, too worn down, and too defeated to imagine them for themselves.

Chapter 3

The Power of Modeling Mentorship

Leadership is lifting a person's vision to higher heights, the raising of a person's performance to a higher standard, the building of a personality beyond its normal limitations.

—Peter F. Drucker

There are two ways to make an impact. One is to run into someone, the other is to lead them—and carry them if necessary. Fourteen-year-old Hunter Gandee chose to lead and to carry. Wanting to raise awareness about cerebral palsy, the teen walked forty miles with his brother, a cerebral palsy victim, strapped to his back. Hunter determined to put a face on the muscular disorder by carrying seven-year-old Braden from a starting point in Temperance,

The coaching paradigm
is twenty-first-century
leadership at
its best.

Michigan, to the University of Michigan campus in nearby Ann Arbor.

The walk was strenuous, and Hunter fought fatigue, extreme heat, and then rain to carry the fifty-pound boy. He said he thought about quitting after thirty miles, but a phone call from a friend convinced him to go on. During the call, the friend prayed with him, strengthening him in spirit. Afterward, Hunter and Braden rested, changed Braden's position on his back to prevent additional chaffing, and then continued the walk.

Family members and friends waited at the destination point at the top of a hill on the campus. The finish line was a large banner that read "GO BLUE!" When Hunter and Braden reached the top, Hunter lifted his young brother so he could touch the banner. Hunter was interviewed about the trek and said, "We pushed through it. And we're here!"[1]

The story is a vivid illustration of leadership. Leaders 1) envision the finish line; 2) carry others on their shoulders; 3) fight through adversity to reach a destination goal; 4) are strengthened by the encouragement of others, even as they encourage; 5) make midcourse adjustments; and 6) when they reach the goal, they share their win with others.

Leaders lead by *principle* and coach by *application*. They develop the team as they journey with them to the organizational destination. If you are in a place of leadership, you are a designated coach. That is both an awesome responsibility and an awesome opportunity!

The coaching paradigm is twenty-first-century leadership at its best. What are its objectives?

- It focuses on training players.
- It builds winning relationships.

Then Moses spoke
to the LORD saying,
"Let the LORD…set
a man over the
congregation…that the
congregation of the
LORD may not be like
sheep which have no
shepherd." And the
LORD said to Moses,
"Take Joshua the son of
Nun with you, a man in
whom is the Spirit."

Numbers 27:15-18 (NKJV)

- It gives and receives feedback.
- It monitors performance.
- It motivates to win.

Former Coca-Cola president Jack Stahl gives an overview:

> I cannot emphasize enough how necessary it is for you to coach the people you believe have strong potential for your organization, encouraging them early in their careers to seek a variety of jobs and projects, where they have the opportunity and enough time in each role to learn the core skills that will be critical to achieving success throughout their careers.[2]

Characteristics of Successful Leader-Coaches

They are good managers of their time and resources.

They have a sense of mission.

They have the ability to help teams focus.

They see their coworkers as teammates.

They work from a game plan.

They position team members according to their strengths.

They define team expectations.

Four Aspects of Coaching

I think at least four words describe the scope of coaching: *leading, mentoring, relating,* and *training.* Let's unpack each of those.

Few things help an individual more than to place responsibility upon him, and to let him know you trust him.

—Booker T. Washington

1. Leading

People do what people see. The adage, "Leadership is caught, not taught," is as much of a classic as a '57 Chevy, but I would suggest that *both* the catching and the teaching have a part in leadership development. Leadership characteristics are usually mirrored in the lives of those whom a leader leads.

One of my leadership heroes is Melvin M. Maxwell, former college president, professor, author, and father of John C. Maxwell. I've told the story on many occasions that when John and I were in college, his father would take us to Positive Mental Attitude rallies in nearby Dayton, Ohio, to hear some of history's well-known motivational speakers, including Norman Vincent Peale, Earl Nightingale, W. Clement Stone, and Zig Ziglar. They impacted my life with their teaching, but Dr. Maxwell impacted my life with his *living* as well. I first learned to lead others by watching him lead—whether in a classroom, a boardroom, or in the car on the way to hear one of those great speakers.

2. Mentoring

Mentoring is the process of adding value to people's lives. Almost every facet of coaching could be defined as mentoring: *inspiration, instruction, correction,* and *delegation.* But every mentee comes to the table carrying unique baggage. The coach's job is to open that baggage with the mentee's permission and find out what can be used or repurposed to motivate them to excellence and efficiency.

Former IBM manager George Hathaway wrote,

> Every good leader understands the fact that his or her employees are, first of all, human. They have feelings. They want to be treated with respect. They have opinions that

must be heard. They know that they are not perfect, but they are good people who deserve to be treated as such.[3]

Mentoring inspires. A *Fortune* magazine cover had the following quote from former president Bill Clinton: "More people can be great leaders than think they can, but they need a purpose greater than themselves."

A mentor affirms a mentee's strengths, sometimes in the face of their denial. My friend Ron McClung blogged the story of Willie Mays, who began his baseball career with only one hit in his first twenty-six at bats. Mays's manager, Leo Durocher, once found him in the dugout, crying after a poor batting performance. When Durocher asked Mays what was the matter, the baseball legend said he belonged in the minor leagues, not the majors. McClung said Durocher put his arm around the discouraged player and replied, "As long as I'm manager of the Giants, you'll be my centerfielder."[4]

Mays went on to hit over six hundred home runs in the stellar career that followed. He simply needed a mentor who believed in him and was willing to let him know it. Johann Wolfgang von Goethe said, "Treat people as if they were what they ought to be, and you may help them to become what they are capable of being."[5]

Mentoring instructs. Mentors are teachers. They relate and motivate by sharing knowledge. Willie Mays didn't become a home run king by the compliment alone, however. You can be sure that even as his coach affirmed his place on the major league team, he had a training regimen in mind. Telling someone *what* to do, without knowing whether or not they know *how* to do it, isn't real leadership.

Mentoring corrects. The twenty-first century has seen epic upheavals in the world of sports. Professional athletes are privileged with large salaries and benefits, but the paychecks haven't seemed to calm the beasts of inner greed and anger. Such organizations as the NFL have had to deal firmly with players that have crossed the boundaries of acceptable behavior.

The front-line soldiers in dealing with errant athletes are their coaches. Behind the locker-room doors and in their private offices, coaches use their parenting skills along with their leadership skills. The results are often announced in minimalistic sentences, such as "We had a discussion about that" or "I think we're clear about that." Both suggest that the coach got his or her point across to the player.

Mentors know that unacceptable behavior cannot be accepted. They kindly but firmly and privately...

- Gather the facts.
- Explore the motives.
- Address the specific issue.
- Reinforce organizational values.
- Explain the alternatives.
- Expect corrected behavior.
- Affirm corrected behavior.

Mentoring delegates. Mentoring allows mentees to learn by doing. In his book *Simply Rich*, Amway cofounder Rich DeVos explains that his family has a private holding company apart from Amway that was created to formally pass along business principles and ethics to its next generation of leaders. At age sixteen, DeVos family members are inducted into the private company, and at twenty-five, they become voting members. Its "constitutional" activities include required leadership and family values training.

DeVos said, "We are very intentional about trying to come together, meet together, spend time together multi-generationally, and involve and engage future generations at appropriate times in the affairs of the family, as well as the activities of the business."[6]

3. Relating

Have you ever noticed that a puppy can relate to just about anyone? Puppies may be awkward. They may be a bit sloppy. They may be impulsive. They may not know how to react to some situations. But put a puppy in a crowd of even the most sophisticated people and their inner child will emerge faster than the puppy's bark.

I've always thought that a puppy could teach leaders and coaches a thing or two about relating to people.

Puppies are glad to see you. They're not concerned about where you've been or what you've done, they just care that you are with them. Coaching is about celebrating people as they are and where they are. When your mentees know that you are more concerned with their *presence* than their past, you have already begun to relate and motivate.

Puppies don't have hidden agendas. Puppies give without expecting anything in return. The wag of the tail, the sloppy kiss, the jumping up to greet you—none of that will cost you. If you want to truly relate to others as a leader-coach, get rid of any hidden agendas.

I like the story of the young lady who broke up with her boyfriend and later had a change of heart. She wrote to him, "Dear Fred, I've been so upset since our breakup that I haven't been able to eat or sleep or watch TV, or even spend time on Facebook. The more I think about our relationship, the more I realize how important you are to me. Can you ever find it in your heart to forgive me…?"

The PS at the end of the letter said it all: "BTW, congratulations on winning the lottery! See ya soon! Hugs and kisses, Alice."

Puppies aren't concerned with your accomplishments. Puppies don't love you because of your degrees or honors; they love you for who you are. Coaching that relates doesn't choose favorites. It is culturally blind and decidedly inclusive. Hathaway said, "Do your very best not to act in a way that signals your preference for one employee over another. Small steps like remembering to alphabetize all distribution lists will keep everyone guessing."[7]

Puppies are loyal. Puppies will love you whether you feed them gourmet dog food in a designer dish or table scraps on a paper plate. They don't practice conditional loyalty—and neither should the leader-coach. If you want to relate to people, they must know that you are unconditionally loyal—that you'll be the first in and the last out in times of adversity.

Puppies are enthusiastic. Everything a puppy does is done with enthusiasm. And that's one of the things that draws people to them. Of course, they can be overzealous at times, but we're all glad that they err on the zealous side. Enthusiasm is a *great* motivator! Teach enthusiasm by your enthusiasm, and watch how quickly people catch it.

4. Training

Forbes magazine researched corporate spending on training in 2014. Its results: "US spending on corporate training grew by 15% last year (the highest growth rate in seven years) to over $70 Billion in the US and over $130 Billion worldwide."

Why the increase? The article explains, "Organizations today suffer from a 'skills supply chain' challenge. Not only do more than 70% of organizations cite 'capability gaps' as one of their top five challenges, but many companies also tell us that it takes

3-5 years to take a seasoned professional and make them fully productive."[8]

No matter the size of your organization—or your budget—you simply can't afford to postpone training. Coaches have an opportunity to relate to and motivate others through an intentional training regimen. From my experience, I believe that regimen must incorporate at least three key areas: 1) values and ethics, 2) attitude and interpersonal relationships, 3) planning and communications, and 4) technique and service.

Values and ethics. One of the most important things a coach can convey is that every worker or leader stands on the shoulders of others. They are a product of the environment in which they were trained. They are here because they own the organization's basic beliefs and best practices. Bestselling author and teacher Dave Ramsey outlined seven life lessons he learned from the late Chick-fil-A founder, Truett Cathy:

- Define your values and stick to them.
- A little customer service goes a long way.
- Make family a priority.
- Know why you exist.
- Plan ahead.
- Invest in others.
- Don't be afraid to start small.[9]

Cathy focused on things that never change. Ramsey cites the founder's commitment to his restaurants' Sunday closing policy as a day of rest and to honor the Lord's Day. You can be sure that every company trainee is introduced to the policy/values from the very beginning.

Ethical practices come from the organization's value system. Those predetermined boundaries give leaders and managers security, but they also give them an obligation to pass the information on through the ranks.

Attitude and interpersonal relationships. Joining a team doesn't necessarily make you a team member. Someone can join a team legally and physically without joining it emotionally. A coach's responsibility is to develop team loyalty—helping people make the emotional connection with their associates. The late comedian Rodney Dangerfield had a slogan that became his brand: "I don't get no respect." One objective of coaching is to teach team members that respect is integral to interpersonal relationships.

The first area of respect is *self-respect.* At the core of good attitude and good interpersonal relationships is a healthy opinion of self. A coach-led, personal-skills evaluation can go a long way in helping team members discover what they *can do.* Once a person is on the road to "healed thinking," they can be taught to respect others.

In my book *ReThink Your Life*, I talk about the importance of filling your mind with the right fuel: "In order to have healthy minds, we must have healthy thoughts. Just as the health of our bodies depends, in part, on the content of the foods we consume, the fitness of our minds correlates with the healthiness of the ideas we embrace."[10]

Planning and communications. In a takeoff of the classic "teach someone to fish" advice, I'd suggest, "Teach someone to *plan* and you feed them for a lifetime." The long-term welfare of any future leader is their ability to build, launch, and communicate a carefully thought-out vision plan. So, an additional coaching objective is to teach team members how to develop short-range and longer-range plans that will set a *destination* and *direction*. Additionally, they must understand the importance of setting objectives and goals for the journey.

The famous Yogi Berra line, "If you don't know where you're going, you might not get there" is gold-standard advice. Along with that, if you don't *tell people where you're going*, you might not get them to follow you there.

Team members must be taught that they are *messengers of the mission*—that the public audience or stakeholder's buy-in of a mission is dependent on telling the story. In other words, if they don't sell it, nobody's buying it.

Modern coaching is teaching the team to use modern technology and old-fashioned salesmanship to "sell it."

Chapter 4

The Power of a Mission-Led Vision

*Every leader needs a clear mental picture
of a preferred future.*

—Warren Bennis

A man once called a nonprofit organization and asked for the "head hog." The receptionist was flabbergasted by his lack of respect and answered, "We don't have a 'head hog' in this organization. If you mean you would like to speak to our CEO, Mr. Alexander, I can connect you to his office."

The caller replied, "Well, whatever. I've got a court order to give you folks a million-dollar donation on behalf of my Uncle Ned, who croaked last week."

Leaders know the
journey is made
of individual steps,
each firmly planted
in uncharted
territory.

"Croaked?" the receptionist said. "You mean he passed?"

"Yep…bought the farm…checked out of the big Walmart line of life. He was my rich uncle, but he had a heart of gold and wanted me to share a few nuggets with your organization. So if you folk are interested in a mil, get me to the head hog."

"Oh, in that case, please hold while I get ol' Porky on the line."

Every organization has an obligation to its constituency—extended or immediate. Its vision is about them, whatever their background. The leader's duty is to give them a promising future for their investment.

Developing a Vision Plan

A history professor commented on Christopher Columbus's discovery of America. He told his class there were three significant aspects of the trip: One, before he left, he didn't have a clue where he was going; two, when he arrived, he didn't have a clue where he was; and three, when he got ready to leave, he didn't have a clue how to get back home.

From the back of the room, an economics major spoke up, "And four, he didn't have a clue how he was going to pay back that loan to the government!"

Strategic planning is the process of clarifying a direction for the future (a vision plan) and formulating specific, measurable actions that will move it toward that vision. It is a necessary process for every organization that seeks to make its mark in today's culture.

In my book *Stan Toler's Practical Guide for Leading Staff*, I talk about how a vision affects priorities:

> When you declare your vision, it becomes a matter of record. Your vision affects the goals you want to reach, the

records you want to break, and the finish lines you want to cross. A challenging goal tends to motivate us. First, we make the goal; then the goal makes us as it pulls us toward it.[1]

Michael Dell, founder of Dell Computer, reflected on the vision of his company in an interview with Jon Swartz for *USA Today*:

> "The world got enamored with smartphones and tablets," Dell says. "But what's interesting is those devices don't do everything that needs to be done. Three-D printing, virtual-reality computing, robotics are all controlled by PCs. Productivity is grounded in the PC.
>
> "Where does the computing power come from?" Dell continued, leaning forward. "How would you run USA TODAY without PCs? Run a hospital without PCs?
>
> "People don't want products, they want solutions," Dell says.[2]

People...want solutions. The core principle of a developing vision plan is its impact on people's needs. Organizations built solely on steel and plastic and a rigid corporate infrastructure will slowly drift into the sunset unless they have "customer first" and "opinion matters" mindsets.

The Essentials of a Vision Plan

What are the essentials of a vision plan?

1. It Is Based on Your Story

Watch how quickly visitors to a corporate headquarters migrate to the pictures on the wall. Whether displayed in the building's atrium or on the walls of its hallways or conference rooms, the pictures are people magnets. People love to see the past and present of an organization visualized.

Paul A. Argenti and Janis Forman give valuable storytelling advice in their book, *The Power of Corporate Communication:*

> The story can be told through official mission statements, declarations of identity, and any other means of communication with all constituencies. In particular, the main sources that external constituencies will rely on for information about your company and the story you are telling include articles in publications, television ads, discussions about the company with other people (for example, family, friends, and colleagues), and direct interaction with company employees.[3]

Notice the emphases—"constituencies," "people," "direct interaction with company employees." The organizational story is people-friendly.

I love the story of the elderly lady who was standing in a long line at the post office. When a postal worker approached her and suggested that she might try the self-service kiosk nearby, the lady pointed to the postal worker at the desk in front of the line. "No thanks, I've been coming to this post office for the last twenty years, and that fella up there at the desk always asks about my rheumatism."

If the lady in line were to write the story of that USPS branch, she would emphasize its personalized service. Who are the storytellers in the constituency of your organization? What product or service have you produced that has had a life-changing impact on them? Get their story and add it to your overall story.

A vision plan that doesn't plant fire in the eyes of others will not inspire buy-in.

What an organization's story should include:

What vision motivated its founding?

What convictions served as its roots?

What turning points determined its direction?

Who were the leaders who left special imprints on its development?

Are there "skeletons in the closet" that won't go away?

How does its history impact your leadership? [4]

2. It Begins with Leadership

The vision apple never falls far from the leadership tree.

Noted businessman and author Max De Pree said, "The first responsibility of a leader is to define reality."[5] You are the captain that keeps the vision on course. Your values serve as its vessel, your ideas are its mapping points, and your inspiration is the wind in its sails. So, you must know where you are heading.

My friend John C. Maxwell said it famously, "A leader is one who knows the way, goes the way, and shows the way."

There's a classic story that describes the urgency of leadership. Its author is unknown, but its message is always relevant.

Every morning in Africa, a gazelle wakes up.

It knows it must run faster than the fastest lion or it will be killed.

Every morning in Africa, a lion wakes up.

It knows it must outrun the slowest gazelle or it will starve to death.

It doesn't matter whether you are a lion or a gazelle.
When the sun comes up, you better start running.

3. It Focuses on the Needs of Others

Author and speaker Nancy Ortberg told of a favorite scene in the movie *Seabiscuit*. The horse's regular jockey had been in an accident and was hospitalized, so another jockey was recruited for an important race. That jockey sat by the hospital bed of the rider who was familiar with the racehorse, noting tips that would help his ride.

The injured jockey told him that if Seabiscuit was behind, he should try to bring him alongside another horse that had "fire in his eye." He explained that Seabiscuit would respond to the look in the horse's eye and would take off—and win the race.[6]

People motivate people. A vision plan that doesn't plant fire in the eyes of others will not inspire buy-in.

- What is the main theme of the plan?
- What felt need does the plan address?
- What overall improvement does the plan offer?
- What is the plan's hook that will draw others to it?

Another question: "Who will ultimately benefit from the plan?" Pat Williams said one of the things that made Coach John Wooden so successful was his resolve to help others. "Some people help others as a way of manipulating them...But Coach focuses on helping people who cannot pay him back."[7]

Nelson Mandela once defined the leader's responsibility to meet the needs of others: "What counts in life is not the mere fact that we have lived. It is the difference we have made in the lives of others that will determine the significance of the life we lead."[8]

4. It Includes Missional Priorities

What are the "to die for" principles of your organization? That, of course, is built into your mission statement. It is the fundamental and undebatable stuff that answers the basic questions:

- Who are we?
- What do we do?
- Where are we going?
- How and when will we get there?

In the classic Sherlock Holmes whodunit novel *Scandal in Bohemia*, Watson is pressed into service to witness the marriage of the protagonist. In a typically twisted turn of events, the newly married couple drives off from the cathedral site of their marriage of convenience in different carriages. Watson's observations of the events surprisingly describe many organizations: "They drove away in different directions, and I went off to make my own arrangements."

A vision without a firm philosophical direction is shallow at best. It can be multidimensional, but it weakens if it is *multidirectional*.

Vision Questions
—John C. Maxwell

Look within you—What do you feel?

Look behind you—What have you learned?

Look around you—What's happening near you?

Look ahead of you—What do you want to accomplish?

Look above you—Who will guide you?

Look inside you—What resources are available?[9]

Jim Collins and Morten T. Hansen wrote, "The factors that determine whether or not a company becomes truly great, even in a chaotic and uncertain world, lie largely with the hands of its people. It is not mainly a matter of what happens to them but a matter of what they create, what they do, and how well they do it."[10]

Along the development path, you may come across a few naysayers hiding in the bushes. Their opinions may be based on the evidence they have gained, but sometimes it will be more circumstantial than factual. In fact, they may try to sidetrack you in the development process.

Daniel Webster gave an opinion during his 1848 congressional speech on adding territories to the US: "I cannot conceive of anything more ridiculous, more absurd, and more affrontive to all sober judgment than the cry that we are profiting by the acquisition of New Mexico and California. I hold that they are not worth a dollar!"[11]

The territories were added. And time has proved the worth of the venture—and proved that not all advice or opinions are spot-on.

Sharing a Vision

Fourteen leaders were asked to share their best leadership advice. *Business News Daily* assistant editor, Nicole Fallon, recorded their answers. One, Cameron Herold, coach, author, and founder of BackPocket COO, advised:

> Lean out into the future. Pretend you go in a time machine, three years out. Write down in three to four pages exactly what your company looks like. Describe every aspect of your company at that time. That's your "painted picture." Then hand that vivid description to your team. Now that

they can see what you can see, they can figure out how to make it happen.[12]

How will you give form to your vision? In Herold's words, hand it to your team.

1. Create a Vision Team

A vision team may be an appointed, four-to-six-member group of stakeholders who will, for an appointed time, hold your organization's future in their hearts and hands, so to speak. They should be chosen carefully based on the following criteria:

- They are visionary—they can see beyond the "what is" to the "what ifs."
- They are complementary—they work well in a team setting.
- They are discretionary—they are able to keep discussion matters private.
- They are cautionary—they are sensitive to organizational parameters.

In one sense, they are your Dream Team. They take the raw material handed to them, refine or add additional material, and help the leader deliver the corporate vision to its community.

2. Agree on a Process

What will the end vision look like? That's the job of the builders—the vision team. But just as a house isn't built without blueprints, the vision will follow some blueprints—a process that will take its components and map them into a completed product.

It will surely involve meetings. Person-to-person, eye-to-eye interchange is vital. Whether that is done through video conferencing,

Rule number one
for vision casting
is to get the real
picture, not the
one that seems real.

through in-house committee meetings, or packaged into a retreat setting, the give and take of the vision team is at the core of the vision-casting process.

Ways to Notice Hidden Leadership Talent
—Mary Jo Asmus

Look harder at those who work for you and scrutinize them beyond their weaknesses.

Look for those who are open and willing to learn new skills and behaviors.

The best leadership-capable employees aren't afraid to step up to a challenge.

Those who have hidden leadership capabilities take decisive action and move forward.

Watch for those who naturally reach out to help others with their work or who seek to collaborate on projects.[13]

3. Gather the Facts

A family with five young children was traveling along the New England coastline in a crowded minivan. Most of the day's refreshment stops had been fast-food drive-thrus, so the father was firm in making the decision for the evening meal: "Sit-down casual dining and seafood—especially crab cakes!"

By the time the family arrived at the restaurant of the father's choice, most of the minivan occupants were less than enthusiastic. As they entered the door of the seafood restaurant, a cloud of pessimism and criticism hovered over the group like an approaching thunderstorm.

When the hostess greeted them, the father asked, "Do you serve crabs here?"

The bubbly young lady looked at the disheveled and despondent travelers and replied, "Sure! We serve anyone! Would you like a booth or a table?"

Rule number one for vision casting is to get the *real* picture, not the one that *seems* real. And that will take a gathering of the facts.

- What are the actual numbers?
- Who are the stakeholders?
- Who are the real decision makers?
- Who are the customers?
- What impact are the products and services really making?

You can't make projections on moving forward unless you have a firm grip on where you are—and where you've been. A look back at the stats, staffing, programming, and production will give you an analysis of trends that can be used in determining your "preferred future."

You will probably need to do a *needs assessment* for developing your ideas. *Wikipedia* defines needs assessment as a "systematic process for determining and addressing needs, or 'gaps' between current conditions and desired conditions."[14]

4. Determine the Readiness for Change

Vision casting's great inevitability is that not everyone will catch it. We have a mini-lake on our property, and one of the joys of being at home is watching our grandchildren catch fish out of that lake.

I don't know who gets more excited (or does more wiggling), the bass or the grandkids, but the end result makes for great memories.

It reminds me of the grandfather and grandson who were fishing. After a long interval of *no* bites and *no* fish, the grandson threw his fishing pole on the ground and stomped off. The grandfather caught up to him and asked, "What's the matter?" The little boy pointed his thumb back toward the lake and said, "The service is lousy!"

Don't be surprised by "lousy service" complaints when it comes to proposed change. Change is a major threat to an established comfort zone. For some,

- Change means they may have to do something they don't want to do.
- Change means they may have to go somewhere they don't want to go.
- Change means they may lose accrued power they don't want to surrender.
- Change means they may be asked to yield a position they don't want to give up.
- Change means they may lose "real estate" they don't want to liquidate.

Sometimes change opens the gate and frees a sacred cow that has been penned in by traditions or opinions.

Mark A. Smith and Larry M. Lindsay address change in their book, *Leading Change in Your World*. They identify four stages of change: denial, resistance, exploration, and commitment, and offer insights for helping people through the process:

- Get them to see that the vision is attainable.

- Transmit the honesty and integrity of the vision.
- Recognize the courage it takes to work through change.
- Cooperate, collaborate, and celebrate every step on the road to change.[15]

5. Write the Vision Statement

You've probably heard the expression "I need to see it in writing." Vision casting, likewise, needs a tangible voice. Once the assessments have been made and the forward ideas have been collected, the next step is to write it out in the vision—carefully, correctly, and concisely. It may be capsulized into a small paragraph, but it needs to be a definitive expression of where your organization wants to be, *and it needs to be put into the language of the constituency.*

In other words, it must *motivate and relate*!

A *results*-focused story:

Shows a culture of optimism.

Shows constancy in purpose.

Shows connection with the team.

Shows creative conflict.

Shows concentration on people.

Shows challenge for learning.

Shows courage to care.

6. Tell the Story

Everyone likes a good story with a happy ending. Your vision is a "happy ending" story. It starts with a compelling history and

Where there is no vision, the people perish.

Proverbs 29:18 (KJV)

promises an inspiring future. In between are the steps that should be taken to combine the best of past and present and turn it into preferred future.

Whether you tell the story in print or in some other media, it must be presented in an attractive, interest-grabbing, and *relational* way. Your audience wants to know how your vision will affect people—not how it will promote your corporation or organization.

- Include satisfied constituents in the story.
- Include founders or their family members in the story.
- Include statistics in the story.
- Include leaders in the story.

7. Gain Team Buy-In

What is the first audience you want to impress? Your team, of course! They carry the banner for the organization. They are the frontline soldiers of your mission. So, they should be among the first to review the vision. They should know where the organization is going, when it plans to arrive, and how they will be involved in the process.

The vision presentation could even be a team event. Make it a celebration—complete with pizza or donuts and coffee. Once you have convinced those closest to the action about the worth of the action plan, you are ready to take the message to the rest of your constituency.

8. Articulate the Vision

Business leader and author Kevin Cope says, "Customers buy more than just products. They purchase trustworthiness,

**Leaders imagine a
future that is better
than the present—and
they look for ways to
make it happen.**

convenience, prestige, or a memorable experience. Determine what *your* customers are buying."[16]

It is one thing to establish the future; it is another to communicate it in such a way that people want to go there—with you. A vision that is carefully crafted and articulated is a way to obtain loyalty from people with a vested interest in the organization. Get them onboard first, and then communicate your vision as widely as possible.

Quality Testing a Vision

The year 2014 may be known as the year of the vehicle recall. General Motors alone recalled over thirty million vehicles. Here's what we should remember: Those products were born from a corporate vision, created, developed, manufactured, tested, and released to the public by the best minds and most diligent laborers in the corporation. But over time, it was discovered that some product components had hidden problems that jeopardized owner safety.

Your vision plan may also be subject to recall. Over time, obsolete or faulty components may surface. Once that happens, it's back to the drawing board. But even before that happens, a second look at the existing vision may indicate some fault lines.

Jack Stahl, former president of Coca-Cola, said, "You and your team must…take into account your organization's strengths, weaknesses, and the environment in which it operates…Develop a clear strategy that will galvanize people and require them to focus on the right actions for success."[17]

So, how does your vision plan measure up? Let's put it through the filter of several criteria.

1. Does It Reflect the Values of the Organization?

As I've said, a vision plan must be built on the foundation of your "to die fors"—raw beliefs that propel your organization. Everyone familiar with Chick-fil-A knows it is a values-driven organization. Chick-fil-A's corporate purpose is clearly seen on its website: "To glorify God by being a faithful steward of all that is entrusted to us and to have a positive influence on all who come into contact with Chick-fil-A."[18]

Chuck Salter wrote about the company's value system, and especially its customer service:

> Every year Chick-fil-A spends more than a $1 million evaluating its service. In addition to traditional focus groups, the company conducts a quarterly phone survey with customers from each restaurant (the incentive: a free sandwich). The 20 or so questions focus on four factors that most affect loyalty according to Chick-fil-A research: taste, speed, attentiveness and courteousness, and cleanliness. Each location receives a two-page report detailing how it's doing in each area and how it compares to the chain's top performers. In other words, what's working and what needs improving.[19]

"Taste, speed, attentiveness and courteousness, and cleanliness" are value standards the company has established to set it apart from other fast-food companies. What are your organization's standards? An evaluation of your vision plan may include a checklist of standards that tell you whether you are being true to your values.

2. Does It Motivate People to Leave Their Comfort Zone?

Dr. No wasn't just a character in a James Bond movie; he might have been the personification of a board member in a church I

From changing times to changing technology, our world is ever evolving. So, a periodic update of strategic plans is important.

pastored early on. "No" was his predictable answer to items on the church board meeting agenda.

Obviously, Dr. No was firmly planted in his comfort zone. A fact of leadership life: If you're for it, you can be sure there will be those who will be against it. That is, unless they can be convinced of the benefits of making a move in its direction.

What are the incentives in your action plan? What components have you embedded in the plan to draw people (particularly stakeholders) out of their comfort zone? They may include:

- added value
- increased revenue
- increased influence
- proven acceptance

Remember, it's a people-driven vision plan. So, meeting the felt or real needs of people must be tested. A sign posted in an eighteenth-century church held a message that will always be relevant: "A vision without a task is but a dream, a task without a vision is drudgery, a vision and a task is the hope of the world."[20]

3. Does It Generate Feelings of Hope?

The third test of vision-plan effectiveness is in its unwrapping. A vision unwrapped should bring a sense of hope. Anyone who has watched children unwrap Christmas presents knows when the gift is on target. It can be seen on the faces and heard in the expressions of those who are unwrapping. There is a "Wow!" factor that can't be explained, just enjoyed.

Watch the same children open a package of clothing, and then compare the reaction to opening a toy. The toy almost always wins.

Friend and church consultant Dan Reiland says, "Mission will give people purpose. Values will give people character. Vision will give people direction." The Christmas package of clothing is practical, and ultimately valuable, but it doesn't have the same hopeful future as a PlayStation or an Xbox.

Why not use the test of expression? Discover how people react to the unwrapping of your vision, at first, and then after a while. The "Wows" may give insights on whether your vision plan is on target.

4. Does It Create Openness to Change?

Sheryl Sandberg, COO of Facebook and former Google executive, wrote a controversial and yet highly regarded book called *Lean In: Women, Work, and the Will to Lead*. *Forbes* magazine contributor, Kerry Hannon, pointed out five of Sandberg's best Lean-In tips:

- Be more open to taking career risks. *Shift from thinking "I'm not ready to do that" to "I want to do that."*
- Skip the people pleasing. *Push back on things, challenging others' decisions.*
- Visualize your career as a jungle gym, not a ladder. *Ladders are limiting; jungle gyms offer more creative exploration.*
- Allow yourself to fantasize about your career. *Have a long-term dream. Ask yourself, "What can I do to improve myself at work?"*
- Start a Lean-In circle. *Form a peer group of eight to ten people who offer encouragement and development ideas.*[21]

Argenti and Forman say a vision "must be re-envisioned, flexible, and responsive to changing opportunities."[22]

Put "windows" in your vision plan—that is, word it (or reword it) in such a way as to let in fresh sunlight. From changing times to changing technology, our world is ever evolving. So, a periodic update of strategic plans is important.

Openness to change is contagious. Once the leader and the team exhibit it, the rest of the stakeholders will be more apt to buy in.

5. Does It Clarify the Cause?

In a book on management lessons learned from the Apple corporation, Jeffrey L. Cruikshank summarized some highs and lows in Apple's planning process. One bulleted summary advised, "Beware of creeping elegance." He defined it, "Don't let your products start to exaggerate themselves."[23]

The lesson can be applied in examining an organization's vision plan as well. If the leadership isn't careful, the plan can develop legs. It can go beyond the established parameters of funding, staffing, facilities, and so forth. Jay Stein, chairman and CEO of Stein Mart, advises, "Grow slowly. We got to 10 stores and said, 'Perhaps we can open 10 more.' Don't wake up one morning and say you want 100 stores, because you'll stretch yourself and your resources too quickly."[24]

When that happens, the core cause often is a casualty. Values are traded for *valuables*. Check to make sure the vision or its revision has not been muddied. Your vision team or other stakeholders may be called to check it for accuracy.

A *Detroit Free Press* article gave a clue as to why identifying "causes" is important to vision casting—especially when a specific audience is identified. The author cites the rising influence of millennials, the 18-34 age group:

> Stores are selling more cause-related products because millennials have a commitment to giving back to society

in some way—37% of millennials are likely to purchase an item associated with a cause, compared with 30% of non-millennials, according to a 2012 study by the Boston Consulting Group…At least 70% of millennials have purchased a product that supports a cause. And they're more willing to pay extra for a product if it supports a cause they also support.[25]

6. Does It Resource a Common Direction?

Everyone who has been in a wedding or has attended a wedding likely has a "wedding story." It's "the wedding party posing on the dock when it falls into the lake" kind of scenario that makes the nuptials memorable. One of my favorites is of the couple who wanted to include a unity candle in their wedding ceremony.

The unity candle ritual involves three candles on a stand, and the bride and groom take two lit outer candles and combine them to light the unlit center candle—symbolizing the unity of their faith and the surrender of their individual freedom. I guess this particular groom had some second thoughts when it came to blowing out his candle, and he whispered loudly to the minister, "Is it okay if we just blow out *her* candle?"

Is everyone still onboard your Vision Express? Or are there those who are hesitant to blow out their freedom candle? Another vision quality test is to see if the stakeholders are still going in its proposed direction.

Following its launch, the impact of your vision plan should be evaluated, not just for its proposed direction but also for whether that direction has been popularized and utilized by the organization successfully.

- Is there an ongoing familiarity with its content?

- Are its principles displayed in the actions of stakeholders?

- Are there watered-down versions circulating?

- Is there a continued optimism about its effectiveness?

7. Does It Outlive Its Visionary?

Author and college president David L. McKenna says, "At each stage of institutional change, the leader must stop and ask the question about matching personal gifts with the management style needed for the next stage of organizational development."[26]

The last quality test of a vision is how it will survive its visionary. Every organization should have a survival plan in place, not only for surviving a calamity, but also for surviving a vacancy. Medicine is doing its best to keep leaders fit forever, but even the fittest aren't immune to a debilitating illness. What is the shelf life of the vision plan once the visionary is on the shelf? McKenna says, "Interviews with great leaders confirm that these leaders speak their long-term vision in general terms, but have a precise understanding of what must be done today."[27]

Do you have a "vision insurance policy"? Not so much for loss considerations, but a policy that assures the longer-range viability of a vision plan?

- What general terms will be preserved?

- What corporate values will be guarded?

- What standards and practices will be passed along?

It's never too late to start planning the organizational transition. Just be sure the vision plan is as ready as the team.

What vision skills must a leader possess to guide a corporation or organization along the path to success? What skills do you need to be a "vision caster"? I'll describe them in the next chapter.

Chapter 5

The Power of Courage in Challenging Times

Courage is being scared to death but
saddling up anyway.

—JOHN WAYNE

Winston Churchill wrote, "Courage is rightly considered the foremost of the virtues, for upon it, all other virtues depend." The most common single quality of leaders is vision. The second most common quality of great leaders is courage—the courage to bring vision into reality, to take action in the direction of their goals.

There are two parts of courage. The first is the courage to begin—to launch, to step out in faith toward your goal with no

Be strong and of good courage.

Deuteronomy 31:7 (NKJV)

guarantee of success and with a high profitability of loss and temporary failure.

The second part of courage is the willingness to endure—to persist, to press on in the face of obstacles, setback, and temporary failure. In both cases, the greatest obstacles are fears of all kinds.

Overcome Your Fears

The greatest fears that most people have are fears of failure—the fear of loss, poverty, or embarrassment. These fears are the greatest blocks to success. Fear of failure paralyzes action, distorts emotions, and causes people to hold back or to make excuses for not going ahead. But there are never any guarantees of success at anything or at any level. Failure, especially at the beginning of any new venture, is always possible, if not inevitable.

Leaders do not like to fail, but they realize that temporary failure is an essential part of the learning process. Business leaders repeat the mantras: "Fail fast, learn quickly, try again," and "Do it, fix it, try it."

Successful people fail far more often than people who are failures do. Failures are so terrified of loss that they try very little, or not at all, and achieve nothing as well. They seldom fail because they never take risks. They never try something new where failure is possible.

As it happens, top leaders are not impetuous or risk-takers. They are instead "risk-avoiders" in the pursuit of profits and business success. The best leaders reduce the likelihood of failure by carefully evaluating every detail before they commit money and resources. They learn every detail of the situation or opportunity. They ask, "What could possibly go wrong?" They then make sure that those things that could go wrong do not go wrong.

Leadership isn't just about reaching a destination; it's also about overcoming some frustrating obstacles along the way.

Confront Your Fears

Everyone is afraid at some level. The courageous person is simply the person who acts in spite of their fear. Mark Twain said, "Courage is resistance to fear, mastery of fear, not absence of fear." The way to eliminate fear and replace it with confidence is to confront the fear head on.

Glenn Ford, the actor, once said, "If you do not do the thing you fear, the fear controls your life."

You develop the quality of courage by deciding exactly what you want, investigating the situation carefully, and taking definite, continuous action in the direction of your goals.

The Iron Quality of Success

The second part of courage, the flipside of the willingness to launch, is *persistence*—the willingness to endure. Once you have launched and taken decisive action toward your goal, you will immediately experience setbacks, difficulties, and potential failure. This is called the "testing time." The "persistence test" is what nature sends you to see how badly you really want to achieve a goal. Remember, difficulties come not to obstruct but to instruct. Tony Robbins says, "There is no such thing as failure. There are only results." The key to developing persistence is simple but powerful. It is for you to make a decision, in advance, that no matter what happens, you will never give up.

Your ability to preprogram yourself is quite extraordinary. By telling yourself, "No matter what happens, I will never give up until I succeed," you plant the seeds of persistence that begin to grow deep inside your personality until you need them. Then, when you face the inevitable setback or difficulty, your preprogramming will kick in, and you will bounce back.

Leaders Never Give Up

Most successful people attribute their success to the fact that they would never give up in the face of temporary failure—no matter what the temptation. Eventually, through repetition and practice, they developed the habit of unshakeable persistence that became a normal and natural part of their character and personality. They simply never gave up.

The keys to leadership success have always been two things. First, get started and take the first step. Second, keep going and resolve in advance that you will never give up.

Orison Swett Marden, the founder of *Success* magazine and one of the most influential thinkers on success in American history, once said, "The first part of success is Get-to-it-iveness; the second part of success is Stick-to-it-iveness." Aristotle said that a person grows in courage by repeatedly doing courageous acts. In that way, courage becomes a habit.

When you practice acting courageously whenever courage is required from you, you will eventually reach the point where you become unstoppable, and your success will be guaranteed.

Why Leaders Fail and Don't Succeed

The story is told of a man who bought his first boat. It was shiny, new, powerful, and expensive. He couldn't wait to launch it and show it off to his friends. But no matter how hard he tried, the boat just wouldn't respond. It was sluggish. It wouldn't plane. He just couldn't maneuver it. He began to look around the boat and to check everything topside. Everything seemed to be working.

Seeing his plight, the mechanic from a nearby marina where he bought the boat motored out to him. Soon the mechanic was in the water checking underneath the boat, trying to find the problem. Immediately he surfaced and said to the new boat owner, "I think I've spotted the problem. We recommend you take the boat *off* the trailer before you put it in the water!"

Publisher and author Michael Hyatt posted "The Top-10 Characteristics of Lousy Leaders" on his highly acclaimed blog:

1. They don't have enough confidence to lead at their level.
2. They're arrogant, assuming they always know what's best.
3. They're disorganized.
4. Their words and actions erode trust, even with their supporters.
5. They over-promise and under-deliver.
6. They don't articulate a clear vision.
7. They don't enroll others in their initiatives.
8. They're not transparent.
9. They're blind to what's happening in their own organizations.
10. They don't hold people accountable—especially themselves.[1]

Learning to Recognize and Overcome Obstacles

I like the story of the executive that had a travel day full of delays and cancelled flights on his way to a corporate meeting in Philadelphia. In addition to the wrecked schedule, his luggage had missed the last flight and was on its way to Detroit. It was past midnight when he finally landed and caught the shuttle for a thirty-minute ride to the hotel. He checked in and wearily made his way to the elevator. Reaching the tenth floor of the hotel, he began searching for his room key. He was still searching when the elevator door closed. He searched his pockets and then his briefcase, but still couldn't find it.

**Coming together
is a beginning,
staying together
is progress, and
working together is
success.**

—James B. Miller

Exhausted, he pushed the elevator button again and made his way to the front desk. "Ma'am," he said to the receptionist, "could you tell me which room I'm in?" She replied with a smile, and then a look of concern, "Why yes, sir. This is the lobby."

Every leader will experience variations of that kind of a day. Leadership isn't just about reaching a destination; it's also about overcoming some frustrating obstacles along the way. How you face your obstacles will determine the impact and duration of your leadership.

Main Leadership Challenges

I think there are at least four main areas of leadership challenge.

1. Unfinished Work

Practically your whole life has been affected by the theme of finishing what you start. If you're like me it started in childhood, at the breakfast table—"Finish your cereal." Maybe the "snap" and "crackle" were already reduced to a hum, but you finished it off and made your way to school. The teacher greeted you with a smile (or not). You settled at your desk, and before long you were faced with the question, "Class, how many of you have completed your reading assignment?" Guilty as charged!

You carried the guilt home with you and changed clothes for some serious playtime. But before you can make your escape, Mother asks, "Did you finish your homework?" And on and on, through college, into your career, you are faced with the same line of questioning.

There are at least three principles that apply to unfinished work:

Principle One: You can do some *things better than* everything. If you push back from the desk, you might see that some of your work isn't an immediate necessity. It may look urgent. But unless it threatens the welfare of your employment or national security, it might be as viable an option for tomorrow as it is for today.

Principle Two: Some of your work is rooted in perceived rather than real importance. In other words, your work journey might actually be a guilt trip. Your plate may have some table scraps from someone else's plate on it. You're doing work for a friend in need. You're doing work to impress another (or yourself?). You're doing work for a perceived reward.

Principle Three: Unfinished work doesn't equal failed work. If it's unfinished, it's simply in the finishing stages. Tomorrow, you'll have a second chance to do what you intended to do today. Reexamine its priority in light of your vision. Change your setting. Think about the possibilities—and begin again.

2. Unmet Expectations

I've met a lot of folks who have spent most of their life trying to meet a secondhand standard. Someone sets a bar that has been inherited from another and then expects everyone under or around them to reach that bar. W. Clement Stone wrote, "There is little difference in people, but that little difference makes a big difference. The little difference is attitude. The big difference is whether it is positive or negative."[2]

You were diligent in framing your vision, identifying your objective, setting your goals, and launching your vision plan. Then, out of nowhere, you take a left hook to the chin when a team member fails or a promised funding doesn't happen. You imagine the critics holding up their scorecards, the naysayers whispering their "I told you so," and your public opinion polls hovering in the basement. What's next? Stay the course.

Author and Fortune 500 consultant Dr. Peter Hirsch wrote,

> Your thoughts determine your feelings, and the emotional
> energy of feelings is a powerful ally…The instant you suc-
> ceed in turning a negative to a positive, that negative is
> going to do its best to reassert itself. After all, it's fighting
> for its life! But then, so are you—and it is really all up to
> you which of the two wins.[3]

In reality, not all expectations can be met. We are living in real
time, with real time setbacks and sidetracks. At times the winds of
modern culture can change quicker than you can adjust the sails.
Political and economic dangers often loom beneath the surface like
sharks with a sweet tooth. The skilled leader will learn to navigate
rough seas by

- consulting the maps
- watching the weather
- avoiding dangers
- making midcourse adjustments

The challenge of meeting expectations calls for making evaluations that include asking yourself several important questions:

- *First, how realistic is my primary objective or goal?* Does it
  have natural explosives built in? Does it really reflect the will
  of stakeholders?

- *Second, what real or imagined fear am I fighting?* In whose eyes
  will I see disappointment if this vision, cause, or objective is
  not successful?

- *Third, is my expectation realistic?* Have I set or borrowed
  an achievement standard that doesn't reflect personal or

corporate resources? Am I reaching farther than my funding or staffing?

Expectations are moving targets, not fixed. They are situational rather than static. If you don't meet a personal expectation, you have not failed—you have simply been thrust into a creative environment where new ideas are born from adjustment, and new goals rise from the ashes.

3. Personal Agendas

It's always interesting to see people unpack their belongings when they arrive for a business meeting. The unpacked items have changed over the years. Once they included a spiral-ring notebook, daily planner, and a Cross pen—pulled from a leather attaché case. Now they may include a tablet, laptop, and smartphone—pulled from an over-the-shoulder designer canvas carryall. But one thing remains: Everyone is carrying a personal agenda to the meeting, no matter what's on the published agenda.

It reminds me of the school board in one town that proposed adding a new chandelier to the principal's office. As soon as the proposal was put to a debate, one of the board members—an elderly man with a hearing problem—angrily stood to his feet and spoke against the project. "I just want to go on record as being totally against this waste of taxpayer money!" he said pounding his fist on the table for added emphasis.

The board member's reaction came as a surprise to the other members. This was the first time their colleague had responded in such a negative and vehement way. There was a long period of silence after the speech. Finally, the board chairman politely asked why adding the chandelier would be wasteful.

Again, the board member stood and took a resolute stance, "Look, the principal only lives a couple of miles from the office. If the teachers can drive themselves to work, so can he. In my opinion, he doesn't need a paid chauffeur to drive him to the office."

The gentleman evidently needed a new Energizer battery for his hearing aid—or hadn't gotten many of the "Word Power" questions right in his *Reader's Digest*! But it gives a bit of insight into what leaders might face when personal agendas sneak into meeting agendas.

How to deal with personal agendas?

- *Politely.* Honey is a better solution than vinegar. A leader's job is always to coat "reaction" with "respect." Kindness is a solvent that soothes friction.

- *Objectively.* What can you learn from the implied or expressed "better way"? Sometimes there *is* a better way to build the mousetrap.

- *Tactfully.* By asking leading questions, you might discover an improved compromise—a solution that will add productivity without dividing people.

- *Firmly.* When all else fails, play the traffic cop and give directions in a firm but respectful way.

4. Focus

Peter Hirsch gives the analogy of a master archer who was teaching his students archery technique. As they prepared to shoot at a distant target, the teacher stopped them and asked what they saw. One described the sky and the landscape around the target. The master told him not to shoot and to put his bow down. The other student said he saw at the center a target and a bull's-eye.

The master archer gave the command to shoot, and that student's

Get the right people on the bus, get the wrong people off the bus, and then get the right people into the right seats on the bus.

arrow flew through the air to the center of the target. Hirsch said the difference between the two students was a "single-minded focus."[4]

Four Common Leadership Mistakes

Hiring too quickly.

Expecting too much.

Assuming you're right.

Failure to delegate.[5]

"Multitasking" may be the mantra of the new millennium. If we can't be everywhere at once, we'll use FaceTime. If we can't do everything at once, we'll use robotics. We have more arrows flying, but our percentages for hitting the bull's-eye are still subpar.

Maybe it's time for an archery lesson: single-minded focus.

Here are some ways to bring focus to your leadership.

1. Avoid "distraction zones." Obviously, there are some environments that detract rather than direct. You know them well. It could be the TV room or computer room at your house, or it may be the break room at the office. You know the distraction dangers that lurk in those places—so avoid them when leadership duties call.

2. Reward yourself. Focus should have an added value. Give it one. When you complete all or part of your project, take a break. It may involve food, it may involve golf, or it may include a shopping trip—but whatever the reward, make sure your mind knows you've reached a "focus milestone."

3. Put your whole self into the focus. Bring your *inner self*, your disciplined thinking, into the process. Spend time mulling the direction or decision away from the noise and the clutter.

Bring your *outer self*—bring your outer interest into the process. Gather your observations of the culture around you. Watch and listen for workable solutions and note them.

Bring your *social self*—bring the ideas and advice of your trusted friends or associates into the process. Learn to leave the authority hat at home and take a friend to lunch just to gain from their knowledge or experience.

The challenges aren't the champions. You are, when you determine to overcome them with your own best practices or the best practices of others.

Chapter 6

The Power of Motivation

*The job of a leader is to get extraordinary results
out of ordinary people.*

—PETER DRUCKER

A s a leader, your most valuable assets are the people who report to you—the people you depend upon to do the job and to get the results for which you are responsible.

According to studies, the average person works at about 50 percent of their true potential. Fully half of working time is spent in idle time—socializing, emailing, taking extended breaks, social media interaction. A primary reason this type of time-wastage occurs is because of poor management or "mal-organization." People are not deployed and directed to contribute their very best work to the company. It is largely a leadership responsibility to ensure that

Therefore judge nothing before the appointed time; wait until the Lord comes. He will bring to light what is hidden in darkness and will expose the *motives* of the heart. At that time each will receive their praise from God.

1 Corinthians 4:5

employees are motivated and feel inspired to enjoy and do their work to their full potential.

To inspire others, you must first be inspired and enthused about the work yourself and must have the right value system and confidence in who you are as a leader. You cannot give away what you do not have. You must then transfer this emotion and excitement to others so that they feel committed and dedicated as well.

The Peak Performance Team

There are five keys to building a peak performance team of highly competent, motivated, and inspired individuals.

1. Select Your Team Members Carefully

Who you choose for your team in the first place will determine 95 percent of your success as a manager or a leader. In his book *Good to Great*, Jim Collins wrote what has now become a staple statement among leadership principles:

> You can't build a peak performance team unless you have peak performance people. The existence of one negative or incompetent person on your team can undermine the morale and the spirit of the entire group.

2. Clarity Is Essential

Each person on the team must know exactly what he or she is expected to do, when it is expected to be done, to what level of quality, and how it will be measured. In addition, each person must know what each other person does, and how each person's work affects every other person.

3. Get Together Regularly

Top leaders are continually connecting with their people consistently to share ideas and to learn about their activity, business climate, and other key business indicators. Top leaders and managers spend 75 percent of their time interacting with their team members—always looking for ways to help them do their jobs better. Alternatively, poor leaders spend most of their time in their offices, busy with paperwork, emails, and phone calls. This is called managing in a silo.

4. Teach the Law of Three

Help each person identify the three things they do that represent 90 percent of the contribution they make to the team that you lead and how it most impacts the organization. Leaders help their people focus and concentrate on those three tasks combined with equipping them with additional training to be even better in those areas. There is nothing more motivating and inspiring than to be fully engaged in challenging, interesting work that makes a difference. A sense of accomplishment is the greatest single source of self-confidence and self-esteem.

5. Make People Feel Important

Inspire others by continually building self-esteem in them. Make them feel important both as individuals and as team members. There are six keys in the formula for making people feel important, motivating and inspiring them to give their very best to the organization. The first five keys all start with the letter *A*.

Acceptance. Each person has a deep-down need to be accepted unconditionally by other people, especially the most important people in his or her life. When you unconditionally accept another person, without criticism, complaint, or judgment, you make that person feel valuable and important, and inspire them to do their best work.

How do you express unconditional acceptance toward another person? One simple way is to just smile. When you smile at others, you raise their self-image, increase their self-esteem, and make them feel more valuable and important. This is why the very best and most productive bosses are also pleasant and positive people, smiling happily at their team members on a regular basis.

Appreciation. Simply say "thank you." Whenever you thank others and express appreciation for anything they have done, they feel more valuable and important. They feel more motivated and inspired to repeat the behavior. The words *thank you* are so powerful that you can use them continually, all day long, and no one will ever ask you to stop.

Admiration. Everybody likes a compliment. Whenever you admire the clothes or possessions of others, their home or office, or anything they have achieved or accomplished, their self-image improves and their self-esteem goes up. They like themselves more. They feel more valuable and important. And because it is you who is making them feel so good about themselves, they like you as well as want to reciprocate by doing an excellent job for you.

Approval. It is said, "Children cry for it, and grown men die for it." Praise and approval are perhaps the two most powerful ways of building self-esteem and self-confidence in other people. In fact, another definition of *self-esteem* is "praiseworthiness." Whenever people feel themselves to be worthy of praise by the important people in their worlds, they feel more valuable and important, and are much more likely to repeat the behavior that was praised in the first place.

Be generous with your praise and approval. Praise people for their accomplishments and for their attempts at various accomplishments. Praise people when they complete a task, and praise people when they complete part of a task. To make your praise more powerful, make it both specific and immediate. Praise a person for a specific action rather than generally. Praise them immediately after they perform the action rather than later. Because you are the leader, any praise coming from you has a multiplier effect on the person receiving the praise. Because you are a leader, your ability to give praise is a wonderful power that you have at your disposal to motivate and inspire others.

Attention. Attention means that you listen carefully to people when they want to talk. Whenever people are listened to by their boss, or by someone who is above them on the ladder of life, they feel more valuable and important. When you pay attention to another person, you are paying value to that person. This is why leaders have a high question-to-comment ratio. They ask twice as many questions as they make statements. They dominate the questioning and let the other person dominate the speaking. Sometimes, the most powerful influence you can have in motivating and inspiring others is just to take time with them, ask them questions, listen intently to their answers, and praise their intelligence and their contribution.

Build and maintain trust. This is the final key to motivating and inspiring others. In annual surveys on what constitutes "a great place to work," trust is the most important ingredient mentioned. Trust is defined by employees in terms of feeling safe and secure at work. As Steven Covey has said, "To be trusted, you must first be trustworthy."

To truly motivate and inspire your people, you too must create a high-trust environment, "a great place to work."

You will notice that none of the actions that you can take to motivate, inspire, and make people feel valuable and important cost any money. What they do require is an awareness on your part of how your slightest word or gesture can raise or lower the level of performance and contribution of the people who look up to you for leadership.

The more you can build high-performing teams of peak-performing people, the more results you will achieve and the more people will be entrusted to you to achieve even greater results in the future.

Motivation as a Vision

Motivation is directly linked to personalization—it inspires people to act and react. Carl Jung said, "Your vision will become clear only when you look into your own heart. Who looks outside, dreams; who looks inside, awakes." When a plan or program or product personally affects you and me, we have an immediate stake in it.

As Meghan M. Biro says, "Leadership is about emotion and great leaders...

have the ability to read people's (sometimes unconscious, often unstated) needs and desires.

welcome new knowledge and fresh (even if challenging) input.

know that what worked in one situation may be useless in another.

> know that talented people don't need
> or want hovering managers.
>
> have a reputation for honesty.
>
> treat everyone with a basic level of respect.
>
> communicate the organization's strategies,
> goals, and challenges.
>
> find out what employees' career goals are
> and help them reach them."[1]

A vision is birthed in the mind and heart. It is a dynamic, fire-breathing dream of something that has never been done (or needs to be done) to increase the quality of life. The visionary/leader is struck with a solution that will make things better. In the short term, it is the tiger on the loose. It roams or sits where it pleases. In the longer term, it is the tiger that has been housebroken. It is trained and on a leash.

The motivation matures.

It is assigned a practical direction.

Those who surround it become acquainted with it—and hopefully will identify with it. Leadership that motivates and relates holds the leash on the tiger. Where he or she leads the vision tiger—and how people relate to it—will depend on how it is introduced.

People are motivated by many things: money, guilt, and recognition, to name a few. But the best motivation is fueled by convincing team members that their efforts have added value—that people's lives will be forever changed by their actions.

Chapter 7

The Power of Personal Encouragement

When you're kind to others, you help yourself;
when you're cruel to others, you hurt yourself.

—Proverbs 11:17 (msg)

A young woman I'll call Helen was teaching math to junior high students, which is never an easy task. By the end of the week, the students were feeling the stress of learning new concepts. Their nerves were frayed, and their faces showed frustration. Some were becoming snarky with one another and with Helen. Realizing that the class would spiral into negativity without some intervention, the young teacher arrived at an idea. She asked the students to list the name of each person in the class, leaving a space between each name. Then, she said, "I told them to think of the nicest thing they could say about each of their classmates and write it down." Students took the rest of the hour to finish the assignment, then turned in their papers. "They seemed more relaxed," Helen said.

Over the weekend, Helen wrote the name of each student on a sheet of paper and listed the positive comments the other students had made about him or her. The following week, she gave each student their list. Within moments, smiles broke out around the room.

"Really?" one student whispered. "I never knew that meant anything to anyone."

"I didn't know anyone liked me that much!" another exclaimed.

Helen was satisfied that the assignment had accomplished its purpose by raising everyone's spirits, and she never mentioned it again.

A number of years later, Helen attended the funeral of one of those students, a bright young man who was killed while serving his country in wartime. The church was packed with Mark's friends, including many former classmates. Afterward, Helen attended a gathering at Mark's parents' home, along with many of her former students. Mark's parents approached Helen and said, "We want to show you something. Mark was carrying this when he was killed." With that, his father produced a paper from his wallet. It was the list of all the good things Mark's classmates had said about him.

"Thank you so much for doing that," Mark's mother said. "As you can see, Mark treasured it."

Some of the classmates overheard. One said, "I still have my list. It's in my top desk drawer at home." Another said, "I have mine too. It's in my diary." "I put mine in our wedding album," said another. "I bet we all saved them," a fourth student chimed in. "I carry mine with me at all times."

"That's when I finally sat down and cried," Helen says. "The lesson my former students taught me that day became a standard in every class I taught for the rest of my teaching career."[1]

This powerful story illustrates two basic truths about encouragement: The first is that everyone needs it, craves it in fact, and treasures it. The second is that you may never realize the tremendous power your encouraging words will have on another human soul. When you encourage others, you unleash a positive power that will far outlive the few moments it takes to speak the words. Your encouragement can change a person's life forever.

Encouragement is a particular form of positive speech that takes your influence to a new level. When you encourage others, you directly affect their thoughts about themselves, their situation, and their future. The results can be astounding. In this chapter, you will discover the explosive power of encouragement and be motivated to practice it consistently in all of your relationships.

How Encouragement Works

Encouragement is hopeful affirmation offered to another person, particularly when they have experienced some form of disappointment, failure, or loss. Encouragement dwells in the middle space between compliments and constructive advice. Without minimizing the reality of one's current situation, it inspires hope for the future.

When someone misses a promotion at work or is denied entry into their preferred university, they will be disappointed. Indeed, they may realize something painful about themselves because of that frustrating experience. However, encouragement does not dwell on that reality but points to a better future: "You'll bounce back from this. I see how determined you are, and I know you're going to succeed."

When a person goes through a divorce, their feelings of rejection, disappointment, or shame may be acute. A word of encouragement helps lift their sights beyond that. "Many people love you, and you are not alone." "You're a strong, confident person, and I know you will get through this."

When you encourage another, you demonstrate sincerity and empathy. When others see that you understand their pain and genuinely care about them, you gain influence in their lives. Please note that this is never done with the ulterior motive of gaining influence. Encouragement, like a compliment, must not be given for your benefit. We encourage others only because we truly sympathize with their need.

What Encouragement Is Not

When offering encouragement, it may be tempting to reach for any positive statement in an attempt to lift another's spirits. That's dangerous because even those who are emotionally low have a keen sense of reality. They know when they're being offered platitudes or unrealistically optimistic statements. When encouraging others, you must beware of offering these three types of false encouragement.

Flattery. Flattery is excessive or insincere praise, especially when given for the benefit of the speaker rather than the hearer. When the boss fails to deliver on a big project, it may be tempting to say, "You're still the best boss I've ever had. This company is lucky to have you!" Some of that may be true, but it will ring false if the boss realizes you're only buttering her up for a promotion or trying to minimize your part in the failure. Don't offer encouragement that you can't stand behind. People long to be shown the silver lining in a bad situation, but they resent flattery or condescension.

Denial of reality. Encouragement is not a denial of the facts, no matter how bleak they may be. On the contrary, it is the offer of affirmation or hope within the negative circumstance. Telling someone, "Don't worry, it'll all work out," after their mother has been given a terminal diagnosis is not sound encouragement. It's better to offer an encouraging statement that deals fully with the facts at hand. "I'll be with you, and we'll get through this together." When in doubt, it is better to say nothing than to appear unconcerned or out of touch with the reality another person faces.

False promises. An offer of help can be a great way to encourage others. It lets them know they're not alone and provides some hope for a solution. However, a false promise can do more harm than good. When a friend has a legal problem, it may be tempting to say, "We'll get to the bottom of this. Justice will be done!" Unless you're a lawyer, that's likely a promise you can't keep. And even attorneys avoid promising to control the result of a legal proceeding. You can offer to seek justice, but you can't promise a particular outcome. You can promise to help financially, but beware of promising to resolve a person's debts. You can offer help to a sick friend, but you can't promise that they'll get well. Desperate people latch on to hope wherever they can find it. Don't make an unwise promise that will lead to further disappointment.

Why Encouragement Matters

When you've just enjoyed a satisfying meal, it can be difficult to imagine what hunger is like. In the same way, when your circumstances are good, it can be hard to understand why encouragement has such power in a person's life. Encouragement matters for at least three reasons.

Life is hard. Life is difficult, and that's true even when there is no obvious crisis in a person's life. We never know the burdens and trials another person may be facing. A popular saying widely mis-attributed to Plato states, "Be kind, for everyone you meet is fighting a hard battle." As if to prove the veracity of that statement, it was likely written by a man named John Watson. A version of the quote originally appeared in *The British Weekly* in 1897.[2] Watson's burden may have been that other people got the credit for his work. How frustrating!

Others carry more profound inner burdens, such as the loss of a child, a chronic illness, an unloving spouse, or the pain of an embarrassing failure. Though they may never reveal that struggle, it can remain with them every day, even for a lifetime. That means nearly every person you meet could benefit from a word of encouragement, regardless of how cheerful they may appear. When you make yourself an encourager, you become a welcome and sought-after presence in others' lives.

Everyone needs affirmation. Second, encouragement is vital because all human beings want and need affirmation. Sure, there are a few folks who act as if they don't care what others think. And there may even be a tiny minority who are truly unconcerned about the opinions of others. But the vast majority of human beings long to be noticed, valued, and affirmed. Even people with normal self-esteem enjoy—and occasionally need—words of affirmation. When you encourage others, you take on a wonderful, positive role in their lives. Genuine encouragers are much loved and highly respected. They become great influencers.

Discouragers abound. A third reason encouragement is vital is that discouragement is a far more common experience than is encouragement. For every positive voice that offers hope, comfort, and affirmation, a person is likely to encounter ten voices that express annoyance, doubt, or frustration. Even if you have a high level of self-esteem, a steady barrage of discouraging talk is bound to affect your spirits. We all need a few positive voices to counterbalance the negative ones we hear throughout the day. Encouragement is like a gentle breeze. You never know exactly when to expect it, but it's refreshing whenever it comes.

Encouragement really works. It produces a marvelous, often instantaneous, positive effect on others. Dale Carnegie observed,

> Tell your child, your spouse, or your employee that he or she is stupid or dumb at a certain thing, has no gift for it, and is doing it all wrong, and you have destroyed almost every incentive to try to improve. But use the opposite technique—be liberal with your encouragement...let the other person know that you have faith in his ability to do it...and he will practice until the dawn comes in at the window in order to excel.[3]

Everyone needs encouragement. When you provide genuine words of affirmation and appreciation, you open a window of hope into a weary soul. You exercise influence of the noblest type, that born of deep concern for others.

How to Be an Encourager

Now that you understand what encouragement is and isn't, let's talk about how to become an encourager. For some, this comes naturally. You may be the type of person who is naturally attuned to the needs of others and liberal with words of affirmation. If so, that's great. These ideas will add to your repertoire of encouragement. Others are less naturally inclined to offer encouragement. They may be less likely to notice when others need affirmation, or have a harder time finding words that offer authentic encouragement rather than false hope. If that describes you, this section will show you when and how to encourage others. Let's begin by learning the occasions when encouragement may be most needed.

When to Encourage

The first obstacle some people face in becoming an encourager is knowing when to offer a word of affirmation or reassurance. Nobody wants to come off as a false encourager, constantly offering pick-me-ups that are unneeded and perhaps unwelcome. The good news is that, other than during an acute crisis, there really is no wrong time to offer encouragement. When someone has just received a diagnosis or is grieving a recent loss, sharing sorrows may be more welcome than words of cheer. People need some time to absorb the shock of their circumstances and to grieve loss. However, at virtually any other time, encouragement will be welcome. Be especially alert for these opportunities to encourage others.

When they struggle. Encourage others whenever you notice they are struggling with their health, in their work or schooling, in relationships, finances, or career—to list a few examples. Some of these occasions are obvious and difficult not to notice. When a person experiences a serious illness, injury, divorce, or loss of a loved one, everyone around them is likely to know about it. But remember that many struggles exist below the surface. How are you to know when someone is facing a significant problem? More often than not, they'll tell you.

Watch your social media feed, and you'll see lots of people sharing their need for encouragement. They'll mention a problem in their family, an illness, difficulties in their relationships, loneliness, and even boredom. Some of those cries for encouragement may be voiced as complaints, but look deeper. And when you engage in conversation with people at work, school, or church, you'll often hear direct statements of their need, though you may pass over them lightly. When others request prayer, express frustration, voice a fear, or even grumble, they're giving clues to the burden they carry. Don't miss those calls for encouragement.

When they're working hard. The next time you're at a restaurant, take a moment to observe your server—not just when they're at your table but as they go about their work. You'll likely see a person who is extremely busy, in almost constant motion, and working extremely hard. Are they unhappy? Probably not. They may love their work and be energized by the dinnertime rush. But expending all of that energy is likely to take a toll. Try saying, "Wow, you're working hard and doing a great job," and see how their face brightens. Anyone engaged in a difficult task is a candidate for encouragement, even though they may appear to have everything under control.

Be aware of the effort that others expend in other contexts as well. Notice the effort your spouse puts into earning a living, parenting, and maintaining your home. See the effort it takes for your children to complete homework, athletic training, or music practice. Observe the concentration and focus of a coworker who is pushing hard to meet a project deadline. Any of them may be like a waiter at a restaurant—not unhappy but becoming tired, and happy to be affirmed for their hard work. Encourage those who are working hard in any pursuit.

When they fail. Failure is not unlike the other kinds of struggles mentioned earlier, but it carries an added feature. Those who fail experience not only a sense of loss but also a sense of shame or responsibility. That can be true in a business failure, the failure of a project, the loss of a game, a divorce, a bankruptcy, and in countless other situations when the result was not the one hoped for. The sense of personal embarrassment or shame heightens the need for encouragement in the wake of a failure. To make matters worse, when a person fails, their pride may hinder them from seeking the community and camaraderie in which encouragement naturally flows. Be alert to those around you who have experienced failure. They are ripe for encouragement.

Whenever. Remember, everyone you meet is facing a hard battle, though you may not be aware of it. Though they may show no signs, most people have a deep inner struggle, burden, or need that causes them to welcome, even crave, the affirmation of others. Don't wait for a specific need. Be an all-purpose encourager. Be willing to affirm others in any and every situation.

Types of Encouragement

"But I don't know what to say." That may be the most common objection to offering encouragement. Some folk are not adept with words, and they struggle to know what to say to someone who has been through a divorce or lost a loved one or is facing a personal crisis. Realizing that flattery and false hope are unwelcome, they fear saying anything at all. When you are stuck for words, consider offering encouragement in one of the following categories.

Personal affirmation. You may not know what to say about a situation, and you certainly can't make predictions about the future. But you can always say something kind about the individual. "I really like you." "You're a good person." "You've been a good daughter." "You have done well." If offered sincerely, any positive statement about another person will be both welcome and encouraging. Everyone wants and needs to be appreciated, regardless of the situation they face. This may be the simplest and easiest type of encouragement to offer because every person has value, and each person can be affirmed for the good within them.

Acknowledgment of effort. When I was young, my baseball coach Frank Ramsey understood the power of encouragement as a motivator. While some coaches yelled loudly and berated their players for mistakes, he always found something positive to affirm in a player, even when giving correction. "Great swing! Just remember to keep your feet planted." "You've got a great arm; now we have to work on your control." "Good hustle! We'll get 'em next time." Being acknowledged for what they did right made the players more willing to hear correction and more eager to try again.

When someone has tried and failed, affirm the effort. You're not giving absolution or ignoring their shortcomings. You're simply acknowledging the sweat and struggle they expended. You're pointing to the good they did rather than dwelling on what they failed to do.

Words of hope. Hope is what any discouraged person longs for. They're dying to know if things will be okay, whether they have a future. You may not have the answer to their specific questions, but you can offer hope based on eternal truths. The sun actually will come up tomorrow. The world will continue to turn, the seasons will change, and life will go on. Simply being reminded of this can bring hope in the face of disappointment. And in some cases, you may be able to offer even more concrete hope based on your knowledge of the situation. While you must avoid minimizing the loss or frustration that a person is experiencing, you can offer words of hope like these:

"You're a young person, and I believe you can bounce back from this."

"In a year from now, your life may be in a very different place."

"People won't remember your failure as much as that you tried your best."

"Tomorrow is another day, and we can try again."

Encouragement always looks to the future. Words of hope are encouragement in one of its most powerful forms.

Presence. There are times when words are hard to come by and unnecessary. Your presence at certain key times in life is an encouragement all by itself. Visiting a hospital, attending a funeral, stopping by after work, hanging out on a Saturday—each of these gestures may be an encouragement to others regardless of the words exchanged, if any at all.

Ways to Encourage

Just as there are several types of encouragement, and each may fit slightly better in one situation more than another, there are also various ways to offer encouragement. The first way we think of is through words of affirmation. Yet there are other ways, including nonverbal ways, to encourage a person. And even when we use words, there are a variety of ways to deliver them. Let's think about some of the ways in which you might encourage another person.

Casual comments. Encouragement often takes the form of words, but those words need not be formal or rehearsed. In fact, the more purposeful we are in crafting words of encouragement, the harder it may be to deliver them with sincerity and authenticity. The most welcome words of encouragement are often delivered off the cuff: "Great job!" "Nice try." "I'm praying for you." Don't wait for a formal occasion to encourage a friend. You can do this in the moment. Offer encouragement right on the spot, as soon as you notice the opportunity. As long as your words are sincere, they need not be well rehearsed.

Public praise. Few things are more encouraging than to be singled out in a positive way among family, friends, or peers. When you have the opportunity to encourage someone in front of others, that praise or affirmation will carry double the weight. When a coworker returns to work after an illness, you can publicly welcome her, say how much she has been missed, and express hope for the team's success with her back on the job. When your team has lost a contest, it will hearten the players to hear their valiant effort affirmed out loud. Encouragement regarding sensitive matters must be delivered privately, but personal affirmation and acknowledgment of effort can often be delivered in public. Correct privately, praise publicly. Remember that rule and your words of affirmation will always be welcome.

Handwritten notes. A casual word is always helpful, but a handwritten note can become a valued keepsake, delivering encouragement for days or even years to come. Several years ago a woman wrote to an advice columnist to express her appreciation for those who sent notes of encouragement when she faced a devastating crisis. She said, "When I began to receive notes of comfort and encouragement, I discovered how remarkable the healing power of true friendship can be. Please tell your readers that any show of concern will help. The simple sentence, 'I'm sorry about your trouble,' says it all."

The columnist responded, "Many people are inclined not to say anything for fear they will cause embarrassment or open old wounds. Wrong. A word of compassion and encouragement is always appreciated."[4] And when that word of encouragement is written by hand, it may be even more appreciated because of the extra effort required to deliver it.

Electronic communication. Electronic media has the tremendous value of immediacy. They make it possible to deliver instant encouragement to nearly anyone within seconds of discovering the need. A text, email, or social media message that says, "Thinking of you," can cut through a person's loneliness and offer hope. Remember that the ease of such communications may make them prone to overuse. As with all forms of encouragement, e-messages must be authentic and heartfelt in order to be welcomed and effective. Also, because they are so quick and easy to deliver, e-messages may carry less weight than an in-person visit, phone call, or handwritten note. By all means, use electronic communications. But be aware that other channels of affirmation may be needed as well.

Gifts. Gifts can be a form of encouragement that are especially useful for those who have difficulty putting their thoughts into words, or on occasions when more overt communications might be intrusive. Interestingly, the act of giving a gift is the real encourager, more so than the gift itself. Flowers will last only a few days, but the act of sending them delivers a cheerful message that will be long remembered. It says, "I'm thinking of you." A gift of food wordlessly communicates, "I'm here to help." Beyond the words printed on a greeting card, its arrival in the mail will say, "You are important to me." These messages are deeply encouraging and a pleasure to receive.

Nonverbal affirmation. There are many other nonverbal ways to encourage another, such as hugs, pats on the back, affirming nods, smiles, high fives, and thumbs-up. These casual signals offer affirmation or demonstrate concern without a word spoken. Remember that any form of touch, such as a hug, requires a good deal of tact and sensitivity in order to be welcomed and meaningful. When you are alert for them, you'll find opportunities to deliver a smile or a high five many times a day. These are great modes of encouragement for "whenever."

Your Choice

We each face a choice when it comes to encouraging others. We can be alert to the needs of others, sensitive to their hurts and struggles, and offer support for the challenges they face. Or we can insulate ourselves from their concerns, focusing on our narrow channel of interaction with them as a coworker, neighbor, or classmate while ignoring their deeper needs. That's the easier choice in some ways. It allows us to maintain a comfortable distance from the sometimes messy and troubling struggles others face.

Yet when you make the choice to be an encourager, you'll find that something remarkable happens. You gain a network of friends and acquaintances with whom you share life. You receive encouragement as well as give it. You develop relationships that go beyond the surface concerns of chatting about the weather or cooperating on a project. You make friends.

In the end, the choice we make about encouraging others is really a choice about our own character and the type of life we'll lead. Will you close yourself to others, holding them at an emotional arm's length? Or will you dive into life with them, sharing their joys and sorrows, triumphs and failures? Will you be an encourager?

For those who are eager to extend their influence and affect the world in positive ways, that's an easy choice to make.

Bless and Be Blessed

Dan Clark recalls that when he was a teenager, he and his father once stood in line to buy tickets for the circus. As they waited, they noticed the family immediately in front of them. The parents were holding hands, and they had eight children in tow, all well-behaved and all probably under the age of twelve. Based on their clean but simple clothing, Dan suspected they didn't have a lot of money. The kids jabbered about the exciting things they expected to see, and he could tell that the circus was going to be a new adventure for them.

As the couple approached the counter, the attendant asked how many tickets they wanted. The man proudly responded, "Please let me buy eight children's tickets and two adult tickets so I can take my family to the circus."

When the attendant quoted the price, the man's wife let go of his hand, and her head dropped. The man leaned a little closer and asked, "How much did you say?" The attendant again quoted the price. The man obviously didn't have enough money. He looked defeated.

Clark says his father watched all of this, put his hand in his pocket, pulled out a twenty-dollar bill, and dropped it on the ground. His father then reached down, picked up the bill, tapped the man on the shoulder, and said, "Excuse me, sir, this fell out of our pocket." The man knew exactly what was going on. He looked straight into Clark's father's eyes, took his hand, shook it, and with a tear streaming down his cheek replied, "Thank you, thank you, sir. This really means a lot to me and my family."

Clark and his father went back to their car and drove home. They didn't have enough money to go to the circus that night, but it didn't matter. They had encouraged a whole family. And it was something neither family would ever forget.

How to Add Value to Others

People are always encouraged when another person invests in them, adding value to their lives. You can add value to others in the following ways:

When you truly value them. How do you show others that you value them? By believing in them before they serve you. By appreciating them before they appreciate you. By giving without expecting anything in return.

When you make yourself more valuable. You cannot give what you do not have. Good intentions never speak as loudly as good actions. Earn so that you can give. Grow so that you can mentor. Experience so that you can share wisdom.

When you know and relate to what they value. What happens when you are focused entirely on your own agenda? You know little about the people around you. Stop and make others' priorities your priority. Ask to hear their stories. Find out about their hopes and dreams. Make their success part of your mission.

When you do things that God values. When your life is done, what will you have lived for? Everything on earth will eventually turn to dust—including you. Give yourself to things that will live on beyond your lifetime.

Chapter 8

The Power to Transform

The best leaders are those who can inspire others to reach for something greater than themselves.

—Stan Toler

A kindergartner burst through the front door of his house. He tossed his backpack in one direction and his lunch in another. His mother took it all in and, like most mothers, imagined the worst. "Scotty, did you have a problem at school today?"

The little boy beamed with enthusiasm. "No, Mom! I had an awesome day!"

Relieved that he hadn't eaten someone's lunch or spent any time at the police headquarters, she said, "Well, let's hear about it."

"Mom, I learned how to measure the distance on a road map. Isn't that totally awesome!"

Do not conform to the pattern of this world, but be transformed by the renewing of your mind. Then you will be able to test and approve what God's will is—his good, pleasing and perfect will.

Romans 12:2

Mom replied, "It totally is! Now what are you going to do with all that learning?"

The boy paused to think about the question. Finally, the answer filled the room. "I got it! The next time we take a vacation trip, I'll read the map and tell you the how-fars!" Then his volume lowered and he said, "Mom, don't worry. I'll still need you to tell me the where-tos."

Effective leadership is more than learning the how-fars; it also includes the where-tos. It helps others complete the journey. It helps them to...

- feel better about themselves
- be more established in their value system
- have more confidence in their skills
- be more confident in the leadership of others
- be more confident in their own leadership
- feel more comfortable in their interpersonal relationships

In other words, it *transforms* them.

According to Wikipedia, the transformational leadership model was introduced by James MacGregor Burns, and "inspires followers to change expectations, perceptions, and motivations to work towards common goals...based on the leader's personality, traits and ability to make change through example, articulation of an energizing vision and challenging goals."[1] Bernard M. Bass expanded upon Burns's original ideas, defining transformational leadership in terms of the impact that it has on followers.

Business blogger Pearl Zhu gives additional insight into transformational leadership:

"**TRANS**" is derived from Latin and as a prefix means "across, on the far side, and beyond." "Trans" connotes a bridging characteristic; thus, transformational leaders practice forward-looking, future-connecting thought leadership. Transformational leaders also facilitate a redefinition of a people's mission and vision, a renewal of their commitment and the restructuring of their systems for goal accomplishment.[2]

Janet Lee Reeder quoted from Burns in further defining the transformational leadership model:

Transformational leadership occurs when one or more persons engage with others in such a way that leaders and followers raise one another to higher levels of motivation and morality...in that it raises the level of human conduct and ethical aspirations of both leader and led, and thus has a transforming effect on both.[3]

Transformational Leaders

Develop the vision—Transform the organizations and head them down the new tracks.

Grow more leaders—Develop a relationship of mutual stimulation and elevation that converts followers into leaders.

Promote changes—Inspire others to follow a vision.

Build trust—Engender trust, admiration, loyalty, and respect among their followers.

Self-reflective changing of values and beliefs— Engage with followers as "whole" people, rather than simply as an "employee."[4]

In forty-plus years of leadership responsibilities, as both an administrator and an instructor, I have practiced transformational leadership. When I began, it didn't have the brand, but as it evolved I continued to incorporate its principles in my leading and teaching. And as I continue to learn about it in principle, I have observed some defining principles.

Defining Principles of Transformational Leadership

It Leads with Gratitude

Rich DeVos, cofounder of Amway, lists "thank you" as one of the ten most powerful phrases. He recounts that at the completion of the company's world headquarters building, an open house was held separate from its dedication event. The open house invitation was given to every skilled worker who was involved in the construction of the world headquarters building. DeVos said those invited included…

> the men and women who drew the blueprints, erected the steel girders, placed the brick, installed the windows, built the roof, laid the carpet, and hung the drapes. The founders and executives wanted the workers to see the results of their hard work. They stood in line to shake the hands of the workers, have a brief conversation with them, and say a personal "Thank you."

DeVos said, "People like to be thanked and they *need* to be thanked! The well of kindness can dry up when we fail to acknowledge the givers of gifts."[5]

People want to be recognized for who they are and what they've done.

I think that's a very important model for every leader. The faithfulness of team members in putting the finishing touches on an organization's mission should not be overlooked. Specifically, gratitude should be given...

By expressions of appreciation. Obviously, a verbal "thank you" is the go-to expression—and yet it's often overlooked. You may have been on the receiving end of the grand oversight. You worked long hours, made personal and family sacrifices to complete a project—and didn't receive a solitary word of appreciation. You didn't know it at the time, but you were enrolled in Leadership 101.

How you express your appreciation may vary, but it should always include a verbal expression. Appreciation motivates work.

> Researchers at the Wharton School at the University of Pennsylvania randomly divided university fund-raisers into two groups. One group made phone calls to solicit alumni donations in the same way they always had. The second group—assigned to work on a different day—received a pep talk from the director of annual giving, who told the fund-raisers she was grateful for their efforts. During the following week, the university employees who heard her message of gratitude made 50% more fund-raising calls than those who did not.[6]

By expressions of affirmation. DeVos says another top ten powerful phrase is "I'm proud of you." "Behind a lot of hard work is a simple desire to be recognized as the best in our profession, to be given a more impressive job title, to win an award or see our name in the paper. Everyone appreciates a pat on the back."[7]

When I was a boy in Sunday school, students were rewarded for such things as perfect attendance or memorizing Bible verses with gifts so small they would bring a chuckle today. It might be a pencil, a bookmark, or a glow-in-the-dark plastic statuette. They would hardly be worth mentioning in today's economy, but when my name was called and I was invited to the platform to pick up the award, it was like receiving an Olympic medal. It wasn't the cost or the size of the award that mattered, it was the recognition that I had excelled.

Today's reward in a similar situation might be a coupon for a fast-food sandwich or a 50 percent discount to a theme park, but the principle is the same. People want to be recognized for who they are and what they've done. They want—even crave—affirmation. Transformational leaders know that. They know that affirming their team members might even be filling a void that some have felt since childhood.

By expressions of acceptance. How do you know when you're on the inside track? Usually when someone trusts you with insider information. "I trust you" is another of DeVos's ten most important phrases. When we trust someone, we are freer to keep them informed about the things that matter most to them. Transformational leaders are not information hogs. They are open about the important stuff. Team members need information to do their work; they also need it to feel accepted in the organization.

Transformational leaders always treat their team members like insiders. Matters not deemed confidential for reasons of security are openly shared with them. They understand the team should be first to know when the organization changes navigation, not the last. They know that information is a symbol of security.

20 Ways to Say "Thank You"

1. Send a card or email that says, "I'm glad you're part of the team!"

2. Remember birthdays and anniversaries.

3. Give a mini-perk, like free tickets to the zoo, free car-wash coupons, or a gift certificate to a favorite restaurant.

4. Meet for lunch (on you) and ask, "How can I support your work?"

5. "Sandwich" corrective comments between two compliments.

6. Make a one-to-one contact by phone, email, or in person at least once a month.

7. Send a card or email that says, "Thanks for the great job on this project."

8. Thank staff members for doing things that are part of their job description.

9. Take time to highlight achievements at every staff meeting.

10. Give a staff member a free day off after completing a big project.

11. Treat the team to lunch once in a while.

12. Praise your team members to your superiors—and let them know about it.

13. Give regular performance evaluations, even when there are no problems, and use them as opportunities to offer affirmation.

14. Ask a staff member for an opinion on something that's not in his or her area of responsibility.

15. Inquire about staff members' family life and health.

16. Send a card or email that says, "I respect your skills."

17. Use your annual report to celebrate team successes, not merely report numbers.

18. Ask, "How can I pray for you this week?" and then be faithful to pray about the needs.

19. Throw a party for staff and spouses to celebrate the achievement of year-long goals.

20. In a one-on-one setting, say, "Your contribution has eternal value because…"

It Leads with Resolve

In a book I cowrote with Air Force Brigadier General Robert Redwine, *Minute Motivators for the Military,* the story is told of a World War II slogan that has survived a century. "Keep calm and carry on" was the slogan printed on posters distributed to British citizens prior to the war. Its message of perseverance was intended to warn them to prepare for the anticipated airstrikes—and yet to resolve to go on with their lives.[8]

The slogan fits transformational leadership. Its leaders push forward no matter the threats or obstacles. They refuse to live under the clouds of pessimism and doubt. They stay focused even in the blurring times.

David Allen, author of the bestselling *Getting Things Done* and consultant for many Fortune 500 companies, says we are all born with "a mind that wanders every chance it gets. And one of the places it wanders to most is the To-do lists of our life…While some of that wandering is healthy and useful, much of it is distracting and stress-producing, draining our energy and reducing our ability to stay focused, creative and productive."[9]

This little poem wraps it all together:

> *It takes a little courage, and a little*
> *self-control;*
>
> *And some grim determination, if you want to*
> *reach the goal.*
>
> *It takes a deal of striving, and a firm and*
> *stern-set chin,*
>
> *No matter what the battle, if you really want*
> *to win.*
>
> *There's no easy path to glory, there's no easy*
> *road to fame.*
>
> *Life, however we may view it, is no simple*
> *parlor game;*
>
> *But its prizes call for fighting, for endurance*
> *and for grit,*
>
> *For a rugged disposition, and a don't-know-*
> *when-to-quit.*
>
> —UNKNOWN SOURCE

Greatness is not
about personality;
it is about humility
plus will. That is
where the essence of
leadership begins.

—Jim Collins

It Leads with Servanthood

Transformational leadership is not self-seeking. It longs to serve others. "Rather than looking out only for their own interests, great leaders learn to ask win-win questions like these: What can I do for you? What can we do together? How can this benefit both of us? Learn to ask 'How can I help others to succeed?' and you will succeed as well. A leader who is always looking for credit will soon be a solo performer."[10]

What does transformational leadership look like under the hood?

Its work ethic is people-focused. Whatever the leader does, it always has the welfare of people in mind. Whether the mission is a service or a product, it seeks to improve the life of others.

Its lifestyle choices are humanitarian. Transformational leaders choose their causes carefully, but they usually reflect the conscience of their community. They have an open heart to the needs of others and are wisely generous in their support for relief efforts.

Its interrelationships are solid. Transformational leaders take their associations seriously. They are faithful to their friends and family. They value their colleagues. They interact with their peers. They listen and learn from others. They can be depended upon. James D. Miles said, "You can easily judge the character of a man by how he treats those who can do nothing for him."

Its transactions are honest. Transformational leaders make agreements on the premise of integrity. They keep their word. They deliver on their promises. They meet their end of the bargain. Transparency characterizes their life. They live above the line morally and financially.

Transformation centers on building long-term success through organizational growth, product or service diversification and innovation and succession planning. Transformation focuses on what happens tomorrow.

Seven Choices with the Power to Transform Your Life

Many people trudge through life doing things they don't want to do, working at jobs they don't like, having conversations they don't want to have, and never doing the things they would truly like to do. Though each of them could point to a thousand reasons why they're stuck in a joyless rut, the answer in every case boils down to the same thing. They're held in place by the limiting belief that they don't have the power to choose. They don't try—not because they don't think they can succeed, but because they don't believe they can *choose* to succeed.

The irony of the situation is that by not choosing a more promising job, more meaningful relationships, or more fulfilling activities, they're making a choice. They're choosing to remain exactly where they are. Each day they choose pessimism over hope, self-pity over joy, scarcity over generosity, and many other negative, limiting choices that root them in place. They have the power to choose, but they make negative choices.

In this section, you'll learn what needs to change in your thinking and behavior in order to be happy and successful and to move to a positive future. There are seven basic choices each person makes in life—for better or worse, intentionally or unwittingly. Positive thinkers make a positive decision in all seven cases. These positive choices flow from and reinforce a positive outlook on life. These seven critical life choices inevitably shape your life, your character, and your future.

Here are the seven choices that transform your life.

- Believe it will all work out—choose *hope.*

- Don't take yourself too seriously—choose *humility*.
- Count your blessings—choose *gratitude*.
- Give more than you take—choose *generosity*.
- Be kind to everyone you meet—choose *compassion*.
- Celebrate life—choose *joy*.
- Keep going no matter what—choose *perseverance*.

The most positive thinker in my life was my father. The specific choices he made reflected a positive attitude. He made a deliberate decision to lead with a positive response, or not respond at all. His choice to do this served as a meaningful example that I still carry with me today.

Chapter 9

The Power of Excellence

*After all the cheers have died down and the stadium
is empty, after the headlines have been written, and
after you are back in the quiet of your room and the
championship ring has been placed on the dresser
and after all the pomp and fanfare have faded, the
enduring thing that is left is the dedication to doing
with our lives the very best we can to make the world
a better place in which to live.*

—VINCE LOMBARDI

What was it in his father's background, his upbringing,
that prompted such thoughts as those contained in
Vince Lombardi's speech, "What It Takes to Be Number
One"? Lombardi was the son of hardworking parents who
instilled in him the habits of discipline and sacrifice. At age
15, Lombardi enrolled in Cathedral Prep, a high school run
by the Catholic diocese of Brooklyn for boys who hoped

"The spirit, the will to win, and the will to excel— these are the things that will endure and these are the qualities that are so much more important than any of the events themselves."

—Coach Lombardi

to enter the priesthood. Ultimately, he left Cathedral, feeling the priesthood was not his calling, but the church remained a central part of his life.

His father attended Fordham University on a football scholarship. Fordham was an intense academic environment run by the then intellectually rigorous Jesuit order of priests. The priests pushed him hard to think about the world and his place in it. The Jesuits believed that human beings could perfect themselves through hard work and dedication to excellence. In the late 1940s and early 1950s, Lombardi's father was an assistant coach at the US Military Academy at West Point, where "Duty, Honor, and Country" were the codes of conduct.

Lombardi believed it was these three influences—the church, the Jesuits, and West Point—formed the filter, the life philosophy, through which passed everything he thought, said and did. And it was this filter that caused his father to believe it wasn't enough to be a football coach. He saw himself more as a teacher, a "molder" of young men. He made his name in pro football, but he believed his father would have preferred to coach at the college level where there were more opportunities for teaching and molding.

Lombardi was very demanding of his players and his assistants. As a person, he was the same including to his family members and everyone else who was in his circle of influence. He demanded the most they could give and the best they could give. One thing he demanded above everything else was personal responsibility. To be "responsible" meant being answerable and accountable for one's actions and meeting one's obligations and duties without prodding from a superior. Around him, a person wouldn't consider taking the easy way out. That was simply not an option.

Coach Lombardi held his players to a particularly high standard. They were all gifted athletes who had a responsibility to use their talents to the fullest. In his speeches to players, he would often say, "I will try to make each of you the best football player you can possibly be." He would also tell them often, "I will try with every fiber in me, and I will try and try again." This was the philosophy of a teacher who felt that all of us have obligations we can't afford to avoid.

Every so often, a player with talent but not the habits or work ethic would arrive in training camp. The team knew it was only a matter of time before Coach Lombardi would take the young player on as a personal challenge. Lombardi's mother, Marie, described his molding process best: "When Vin is challenged to try and make a great one out of a ball player, I can only feel sorry for the player. Vin is going to make a hole in his head and pour everything into it. When it starts, the player hasn't any idea what he's in for and he hasn't got a chance. He'll get hammered and hammered until he's what Vin wants him to be. You can't resist it nor can you fight it."[1]

Lead with Excellence

Success is not a zero-sum game. Excellent leaders know that their achievement does not depend on someone else's failure. There is more than enough success to go around. The most effective leaders are not afraid to help others reach their goals; they believe in the power of the win-win situation.

Zig Ziglar always said that you can get everything you want if you help enough others get what they want. In order to do that, you'll have to have an attitude of openness. That may require a change of mind.

No team will follow a truly selfish leader. The team may establish a good work regimen and perform well, but unless the members respect their leader, that team will not excel.

The best leaders display that seldom-seen virtue called humility. They discover real worth in terms of their ability to generate team excellence, not personal recognition.

Here are five marks of greatness in a leader.

1. *Excellent leaders don't care who gets the credit as long as the job gets done.* Actions take precedence over accolades. Goals are more important than gold. Ribbons are incidental to right behavior. Excellent leaders don't draw attention to themselves; they express appreciation for the contributions of others.

2. *Excellent leaders are willing to put the mission ahead of their personal agenda.* They've discovered the greater joy of giving their lives for something worthwhile. The purpose, mission, and objectives of the organization are paramount, while the personality and personal achievement of the leader are secondary.

3. *Excellent leaders are quick to forgive.* Little people hold grudges; big people forgive and forget. Little people nurse insults and look for revenge; big people let bygones be bygones. All great leaders are big people. They earn respect, but never demand it. They avoid petty squabbles and develop thick skins.

4. *Excellent leaders delight in the achievements of others.* Excellent leaders realize that they themselves can never accomplish all they dream; others must carry out their vision. So they invest in others, encourage them, train them, and enable them to succeed. The best leaders realize that there's plenty of success to go around, and they help those around them succeed.

5. *Excellent leaders give credit where it's due.* They know that they are highly skilled, yet they realize that their success depends on the contribution of others. They know there are no "little people" in the organization; every person's contribution is significant. Excellent leaders know how to say, "Well done," and they say it often.

Enjoying great success does not depend on having a great ego. In fact, the opposite is almost always true. Those who think the most of themselves are usually respected little by others.

Former Georgia governor and businessman Sonny Perdue said, "My philosophy of leadership is to surround myself with good people who have ability, judgment, and knowledge, but above all, a passion for service." I agree.

Reaching Excellence Through Seeking Perfection

The level of people's expectations has a great deal to do with the results they achieve. Don Shula's vision of perfection for the football team he coached was to win every game. Was that possible? No. But the 1972 Miami Dolphins did for a season, establishing a level of perfection that no other NFL team has ever matched.

Shula's philosophy was that if you're shooting at a target, you're better off aiming at the bull's-eye, because if you miss it, the chances are high you'll still hit the target. If you aim just for the target and miss, you're nowhere.

If Shula's goal had been just to win more games than he lost, do you think he would have recorded the only perfect season on record and become the winningest coach in NFL history? Not so much.

If you don't seek perfection, you can never reach excellence.

A Standard of Excellence

The word *competent* sometimes gets used to mean "barely adequate." The root meaning of competence means "complete." Competent leaders have everything they need to do the job of leading people and do it well. Leaders who are highly competent have some things in common:

- *They are committed to excellence.* John Jonson in *Christian Excellence* writes, "Success bases our worth on a comparison with others. Excellence gauges our value by measuring us again our own potential."
- *They never settle for average.* The word *mediocre* literally means "halfway up a stony mountain." Competent leaders never settle for average or mediocrity.
- *They pay attention to detail.* Dale Carnegie said, "If you do little jobs well, the big ones tend to take care of themselves."
- *They perform with consistency.* Highly competent leaders give their best all the time.

People don't follow others by accident. They follow individuals whose leadership they respect. And the more leadership ability a person has, the more quickly he or she recognizes leadership—or its lack—in others.

When people get together for the first time as a group, take a look at what happens. As they start interacting, the leaders in the group immediately take charge. They think in terms of the direction they desire to go and who they want to take with them. At first, people may make tentative moves in several different directions, but after the people get to know one another, it doesn't take long for them to recognize the strongest leaders and to follow them.

In time, people in the group get on board and follow the strongest leaders. Either that or they leave the group and pursue their own agendas.

Discover Your Calling

Zig Ziglar wrote,

> If a man is called to be a street-sweeper, he should sweep streets as Michelangelo painted, or Beethoven composed music, or Shakespeare wrote poetry. He should sweep streets so well that all the hosts of heaven and earth will pause to say, "Here lived a great street-sweeper who did his job with excellence."
>
> We could count on one hand the number of people in history whose calling in life was handed to them on a silver platter. A somewhat larger number have had a "Eureka" moment in which they somehow knew what they were called to do for the rest of their lives. But for most of us, discerning our call in life is a process, something that becomes clear over time.
>
> Opportunities are not synonymous with calling. There are more opportunities in life than any of us could possibly take advantage of. And many people never find their true calling because they don't measure opportunities against purpose [and therefore don't] have the emotional and spiritual energy (passion) to sustain the work. Nothing worthwhile in life was ever achieved without a compelling reason to achieve it.
>
> Dr. Howard Hendricks, a well-known professor of theology and leadership coach, said, "Your career is what

you are paid for, your calling is what you are made for. The goal is to have your career and your calling overlap as close to 100 percent as possible so you get paid to do what you were made to do. Some rare individuals start at 100 percent overlap, but most begin somewhere below 50 percent and spend a few years closing the gap between career and calling."

For instance, if your heart's desire is to travel the world, there are plenty of jobs that can help you achieve your dream. Working for an airline is possibly the most obvious. Working for an insurance company assessing property damage from natural disasters, or even being a missionary, will take you places even you never considered.

Why be involved in anything that does not help you accomplish your life purpose? Therefore, a key question to ask is: What really matters to you? What do you do when you have free time? What do you dream about doing when you have idle thought time to just think? Whatever it is, that's where your heart is; that's what you're passionate about. And somewhere, connected to that passion, is your calling.

We need to become attuned to those moments in life that reveal our values and our passion. It's one thing to identify those moments and take note of what they are saying to you, but it's another to respond to them and to use those moments as a launching pad for action. Sometimes you may not like what you learn about yourself, and that's important too. The important thing is to have your radar on and be in touch with what your heart is telling you about who you are and what fulfills you—and what doesn't—on a daily basis.

Even if we are content in what we are doing, we should be continually looking for ways we can make an uplifting contribution to our world. We should be asking questions like, What is it that leaves my heart feeling full and my spirit at peace? How can I use my gifts and abilities in a productive and profitable way? How can I move beyond my current level of abilities to make an even greater contribution in the future? What new interests or challenges have come into my life lately that I need to pay attention to? Could they be doorways or pathways to a new and more fulfilling calling? Am I sensitive to things happening around me—those divine connections—that could be signposts or wake-up calls? To what degree am I already fulfilling the highest calling for my life of which I am currently aware?

Think about what makes your heart truly glad. Then think about the world's needs. To what degree is there convergence between the two? Man's greatest calling comes when he discovers and confirms that what he was put on this earth to do is meeting a genuine need for other people. We discover value and satisfaction in our calling when we can honestly say, "There is nothing I would rather do." The sense of "deep gladness" you get from fulfilling your calling both inspires and energizes you to continue onward to excellence regardless of the personal cost.

Think back on the happiest moments in the tapestry of your life. In the thousands of moments that are woven together to make up your story, there are undoubtedly some where time seemed to stand still; where you felt as though you were outside yourself, watching yourself doing something truly significant, truly gratifying, truly important. I believe those are the moments in which you find yourself standing at the crossroads of purpose, passion, and peak performance, where those three dynamics merge and become one. [2]

Leading with Values

Leaders hold the keys to the "Values Gate." Like it or not, the ethical nature of an organization is under their watch. Former president George H.W. Bush gave some practical, value-laden advice to such leaders:

> *First*, no matter how hard-fought the issue, never get personal…
> *Second*, do your homework. You can't lead without knowing what you are talking about…
> *Third*, the American legislative process is one of give and take. Use your power as a leader to persuade, not intimidate…
> *Fourth*, be considerate of the needs of your colleagues, even if they're at the bottom of the totem pole.[3]

Leaders need all the advice they can get—and sometimes get more than they want! But as captain of the organizational vessel, you are responsible to…

- chart the course
- recruit and motivate the crew
- secure the cargo
- keep the vessel on course until it reaches the destination

You are also responsible to keep it up to code, to make sure it passes moral inspection by its constituents. The values of your "vessel" are most often a reflection of your personal values. So great caution should be taken to make sure your organization stands tall in its community. How?

1. Stay on track. More than likely you have taken time to construct a statement of purpose—documenting the whats, the whys, and the wherefores of your organization. Your next important task will be to keep your organization and its products or services on that purpose track.

2. Don't advertise something you can't deliver. The integrity of many organizations has been tarnished by 100-dollar ads for 10-dollar programs. If you can't deliver the "best," "biggest," or "most spectacular" output on the face of the earth, then don't promise it.

3. Treat staff with respect. As someone once said, "You're not only known by the company you keep, you're also known by how you keep your company." Your encouragement, compassion, training, and support for your staff will soon be well known in your community. (They'll also hear about staff abuse in a hurry!)

4. Be open about plans and programs. Some leaders act like they're conducting an undercover operation. A lack of publicity about organizational programs or plans is a surefire integrity killer. A friend of mine was once invited to be a staff member of a religious organization. When he arrived to begin his responsibilities, he soon discovered that his superior had neglected to tell anyone in the organization about the hire—including the governing board. A tsunami of embarrassment soon covered all hopes of my friend's staff position. And the leader in charge of the covert operation lost his parking space.

5. Keep the financial books open. Stakeholders want to be informed when the cash "flows" and when the cash "ebbs." One of the most important documents that an organization can publish is its financial report. "Workhorses" are skittish.

6. Protect the integrity of the workers. When that new hire walks through the door of your organization, you are responsible for more than their health benefits and payroll. You are responsible to provide a safe environment.

But safety awareness includes more than passing out hard hats; it also includes providing an environment where staff members can work without fear of all forms of harassment, where they feel accepted and appreciated, and where they feel free to contribute to the organization's mission with excellence.

7. Focus on the main thing. Probably your greatest challenge will be to keep the organizational oars in the water, paddling in the direction of its mission. Along the way, you'll be tempted to take side trips or look for shortcuts. Your institution's integrity will also be known by its focus. Can it avoid expensive or pop mission add-ons? That's up to you. When all else fails, stay the course.

Chapter 10

The Power of a Positive Message

Four short words sum up what has lifted most successful individuals above the crowd: "a little bit more."

—A. Lou Vickery

A blind man sits on a city street. Beside him is a sign that reads "I'm Blind Please Help." All around him people are making their way through the streets, some laughing and chatting, others bored and distracted. Few notice the man, and only occasionally does anyone respond to his message. One or two people toss a small coin in his direction, which he eagerly gathers up and drops into a tin can by his side. Despite his pitiable condition and request for aid, almost no one notices or cares.

A well-dressed young woman happens by. She too walks past the man, then stops. She returns to regard the blind man and his circumstances. Without a word, she takes up his tattered cardboard sign, turns it over, and writes something on the other side. The blind man, aware that someone is nearby, reaches out to touch her stylish shoes. The woman replaces the sign and walks away.

Within moments passersby begin to notice the blind man. Most of them reach into their pockets, and coins now shower down about the man, who eagerly scoops them up, filling his tin can with money.

Sometime later, the young woman returns and stands before the man, smiling in approval. Sensing her presence, the man reaches out, feeling the same shoes as before. "What did you do to my sign?" he asks.

Kneeling down, the woman places a hand on his shoulder and says kindly, "I wrote the same. Only in different words." As she walks away, we see the sign as the woman recreated it: "It's a beautiful day and I can't see it."[1]

That fictional story, popularized in a brief video titled *The Power of Words*, became an internet sensation for good reason. For it shows the amazing power of words to influence the thoughts and actions of others. If you hope to influence others with your vision for the future, your positive thoughts must be translated into positive messages. Your words have the power to change the world.

Words are the single most potent means of influence at our disposal. In this chapter, you will discover the incredible power contained within the simple words and messages you speak and share daily. You'll learn how negative words undermine your influence in the world, and you'll find out how to use positive messages to deepen your impact on those around you.

Words Shape Powerful Messages, Perceptions, and Reactions

Words have tremendous power in our lives because they shape how we perceive reality. Words do not have the power to create reality, but they do change how we understand it, and, therefore, how we feel about it and what we do about it. Words are the key to belief, and belief unlocks action.

For example, when you meet someone for the first time, a single word of introduction has the power to shape how you feel about that person and, therefore, how you respond to them. Have you ever met someone you'd heard described as untrustworthy, narcissistic, shallow, or uninteresting? What was your first reaction to them? Likely you were looking for signs to confirm the judgment you'd been given. Even if that description was untrue, it probably took a long time to dispel the notion. One negative word shaped your perception of the individual, making it nearly impossible to see their better qualities. In the same way, when you meet someone who is described as likeable, friendly, or funny, you're almost certain to be receptive to them and give them the benefit of the doubt. Words are the filter that reality must pass through to get into your brain. As such, they have tremendous power to shape how you think, feel, and behave.

It's no surprise, then, that politicians, activists, and marketers vie to define the terms surrounding any idea or product. When passing a law, it makes a tremendous difference whether the public perceives it as a "job killer" or a "deficit reducer." And we are much more likely to buy a product that is presented in terms of its benefits—chic, cutting-edge, elegant, excellent—rather than its drawbacks—expensive, unnecessary, unproven. Words determine how you think, and, therefore, how you respond. They don't create reality, but they certainly do define how we perceive it.

Words have even greater power when applied to people. You've heard the old saying, "Sticks and stones may break my bones but names will never harm me." That adage focuses on the first part of our understanding of words: they do not create reality. A rock thrown in your direction may literally reshape a part of your anatomy, but a name, label, insult, or other word cannot affect your physical well-being; it can't change reality.

That's a nice thought, and it may help some folk to allow insults to roll off their backs. Yet anyone who has been on the receiving end of name-calling or trolling will tell you that words applied to your spirit have the same effect as words applied to any other thing. The words cannot change your objective reality, but they can shape how you perceive yourself. Negative words really can cause psychological damage. Words have the power to shape how we think about the world, our circumstances, and ourselves.

When you communicate messages, either positive or negative, they influence those around you to accept your view of reality. When you disparage an idea, others will think less of it, regardless of whether your criticism is true or false. When you praise a product, others will be more inclined to try it, regardless of its objective benefits. In that sense, your words have tremendous power. They are a potent means of exercising influence over those around you.

To begin using your words as a means of influence, it's important to understand various types of messaging—both positive and negative—and how they impact your ability to influence others. We'll begin by examining several forms of negative messaging that you must learn to recognize and avoid.

Negative Messages that Kill Influence

Most negative messages are merely negative thinking expressed in words. They are your negative thoughts and formulations cast as the most rudimentary form of action—talking. Negative messages undermine your ability to influence others in two ways. First, negative speech is always hostile either to a person or an idea. While it is legitimate and often helpful to offer a negative opinion—saying that something isn't true, for example, or that an idea is infeasible—negative speech often goes beyond that. It can become an attack, often subtle, against another person. So negative speech is an influence killer because it sets you in opposition to the very people you might hope to influence.

A second reason negative messages undermine influence is that they easily become a habit, making you appear to others as a negative person. While it might be true that negative influence is still influence, it certainly is not the influence you want to exert on others. The hope you have for the world is positive. You want others to accept your vision for a better future in your family, workplace, or community. Negative messages may make you a destroyer, but they will never make you a builder. To influence others in a positive direction, you must offer a hopeful, positive alternative to their current perception of reality—not simply undermine the way they currently think. Let's see how negativity undermines your influence in these common forms of negative messages.

Common Forms of Negative Messages

Complaining

Complaining is voicing displeasure over circumstances, particularly about things that are beyond your control. We are all tempted to complain about things (or people) we don't like. You cannot change the weather, so you complain that it's raining when you'd like to be outside. You can't clear up a traffic jam, so you sit on the freeway and complain about being stuck. You cannot change the behavior of coworkers, so you voice a gripe to them and others.

Complaining feels good but is entirely counterproductive. It seems like a positive thing to do because it gets your frustration off your chest, relieving the annoyance temporarily. And it can be a bonding experience. When you complain, others will join you, making your aggravation a shared event. At first, it can feel as if complaining is a positive thing to do.

The effects are short-lived, however, and voicing complaints nearly always produces two negative effects in your life. First, it makes you feel worse in the long run by reinforcing the idea that you are helpless. Complaining about the rain does nothing to construct a positive plan for the day. It just makes you feel trapped in the house. Complaining about a coworker does nothing to address the problem. It merely makes you feel stuck in a situation you can't control. Far from improving your outlook, complaining actually makes you feel more trapped and frustrated.

Second, complaining reduces your ability to lead others in finding positive solutions. For one thing, you are far less likely to look for solutions when you trap yourself in a loop of negative thinking. Remember how negative thinking affects the brain. When you complain, you are far less likely to be able to think creatively and come up with solutions. Not only that, but complaining also casts you in a negative role among your peers. Family members, coworkers, and online friends may find humor in your complaints and even join you for a while, but they are unlikely to see you as a leader. Your ability to influence them in a positive direction will be severely compromised by your penchant for complaining.

Outrage

Outrage is a useful emotion when confronted with something truly outrageous. We do right to be outraged by genocide or the abuse of children or racial discrimination. However, the outrage we most often hear expressed, especially in social media or other online forums, is something closer to the self-righteous condemnation of others. Outrage over gross evil is perfectly legitimate and necessary. Loudly condemning others for their mistakes, missteps, or errors in judgment while ignoring our own shortcomings is one of the most virulent forms of negative speech today.

As Jesus once said, it's the height of hypocrisy to take a speck of sawdust out of another person's eye when you have a two-by-four lodged in your own.[2] When you express rank indignation or outrage over what should be forgivable offenses, you undermine your influence by making yourself appear hypocritical. As with complaining, it will be easy to aggregate a group of followers who are similarly indignant, but they will likely also be hypocritical. To extend your influence, reserve your outrage for the truly outrageous. Be known as a person who is tolerant and fair-minded.

Naysaying

Naysaying is devaluing an idea without giving it full consideration. You will hear it nearly anytime a change is proposed at work, in a school, a church, or any other social structure. The two most popular statements of naysayers are "That'll never work" and "We've never done it that way before," with honorable mention going to "We tried that once and got nowhere."

Naysayers purport to be good leaders because, in their minds, they're trying to save everyone time. What they *think* they're saying is "Trust me, I have this one figured out." What people actually hear, however, is "You're not smart enough to think this through," which is a terribly negative message to give to others. Most often, what nay-sayers would say if they were being honest is something more like this: "I'm so afraid of change that I'm not even willing to consider what you're proposing."

Naysayers may be successful in winning an argument or con-trolling the decision making of a group, but that is a far cry from influence. Real influence is guiding people to a positive outcome that you have envisioned, not simply blocking others from imple-menting their ideas.

Criticizing

Criticizing is demeaning a person or idea without construc-tive intent. This is not the same as constructive advice, sometimes called constructive criticism (more on that later). What I mean here by criticism is tearing others down with no intention of building them up.

It's easy to be critical because other people—including you and me—have plenty of faults. We all make mistakes, do things imper-fectly, overreact occasionally, and get wrong ideas. Almost everyone can see the faults and foibles in another person, so being critical is the easiest thing in the world to do. And it feels good. For some rea-son, we always feel as if we stand a little taller when we're standing on the rubble of another person's work or ideas or reputation.

We don't, of course. And criticism is entirely detrimental to our ability to influence others. When you become known as a critic, people will look to you only when they want to hear the worst about a person, idea, or situation. But since they realize that your judgments are always negative, they will never trust you to provide the way forward.

Gossip

Gossip is criticizing someone who is not present. Gossip may also be defined as repeating negative information about a person—whether true or untrue—without a definite need to do so. Privately warning a friend who is considering a business deal that the other party once swindled you is not gossip. The information is true and you have a definite need to share it privately. However, telling a group of friends that another person's marriage is breaking apart—so you've heard—is gossip. The information may indeed be true, but when shared with no positive intent and to a wider circle than necessary, it becomes gossip. Gossip usually begins with the words, "I heard that…"

Nearly all negative information that cannot be verified may be considered gossip, regardless of the forum in which it is shared. By that definition, much of the news we read via social media might be considered gossip. To avoid gossip, ask yourself these three questions:

1. Do I know for sure that this is true?
2. Do I have a constructive and compelling reason for repeating this information?
3. Am I sharing this information with the minimum number of people required to satisfy my reason for sharing?

If the answer to any of the three questions is no, sharing it with even one person is likely a form of gossip.

Gossip, like complaining, is negative influence. It influences others *not* to trust, accept, or welcome another person, initiative, or idea. A person with a reputation for gossiping is generally considered untrustworthy, even by those who give ear to the "news." Therefore, those who gossip are seldom able to influence others in positive ways. To protect your influence over others, avoid gossip.

Trolling

Trolling is a new form of negative messaging unique to online communication. It is faultfinding and gossiping in online media, particularly social media. Trolling is purposely destructive speech, often aimed directly toward another person. Trolls say negative, often hostile or nasty things to or about others with no other purpose than to tear down their ideas or shame them.

Trolling is easy to do because of the relative distance that the internet provides (online versus face-to-face) and the shared outrage of a group or tribe. Sarcastic comments left on a blog, belittling jokes passed along through social media, "gotcha" tweets and Facebook posts are all examples of trolling.

Trolls have great power to destroy but none to cast vision, influence positively, or provide leadership. If you hope to influence others, you cannot begin that leadership with sarcasm, mockery, or insults. To lead positively, speak positively.

Spinning

The concept of spin has entered our vocabulary through politics, where a politician's surrogates or other pundits will amplify a speaker's remarks in order to "spin" them in a different direction. While it is legitimate to clarify a speaker's intention, the term *spin* has come to mean shading or distorting the truth by providing an alternative view of reality.

It isn't just politicians who spin the facts. A struggling business may spin their situation to a creditor by saying that they are "positioning themselves for success." A deceitful spouse may spin their behavior as "misremembering" what happened. This old story about a political candidate reveals the absurdity of trying to spin the truth. The politician said, "Half of my constituents are for this issue, and the other half of my constituents are against it. I want to make it absolutely clear to all that I am 100 percent behind my constituents!"

Most people are uncomfortable with telling outright lies, but untruthfulness comes in many lesser forms—such as exaggerating, omitting important facts, and making misleading statements. People who spin the truth seldom have influence outside their tribe. In other words, the only people they influence are those who already believe their ideas. If you want to cast wide influence, tell the truth, without embellishment, in all situations.

Positive Messages that Shape Influence

While negative messages are an influence killer, positive messages enhance reputation and build influence. When you become a positive thinker, those positive thoughts will seep out through your words. As they do, you'll become known as a person who is affirming, open to others, and brimming with good ideas. You'll become an influencer. Here are several types of positive speech that will establish you as an influencer of others. While some are the direct opposites of the negative messaging we just examined, many are unique forms of positive communication. Master these, and others will listen to you.

Positive Observation

Positive observation is simply pointing out what's good, right, or hopeful in a situation. It is the opposite of complaining, which voices the negatives. Positive observations inspire hope and opportunity by identifying what's possible in any given situation. Rather than making you feel dour and helpless, positive observations build your spirit and create new possibilities.

For example, if it's raining on the day you planned to play golf, one reaction would be to complain about the weather, making you feel miserable and helpless. A positive observation could be to mention that it's a perfect day for reorganizing the basement. When you're stuck in traffic, you can complain about the inconvenience, making you and your companions tense and anxious, or you might observe that it's a great opportunity to finish your conversation or listen to an interesting podcast.

Making positive observations begins with asking the question, "What does this make possible?" when confronting a frustrating circumstance. If you think about it, there is nearly always some new opportunity hidden within a disappointment. Those who make positive observations are natural influencers, and their enthusiasm for new ideas gains them respect.

Compliments

A compliment is a positive observation addressed to a person. It points out something good, right, or pleasing about them. It's the opposite of an insult. Notice, however, that there is an important difference between compliments and flattery. Flattery is false or inflated praise given for the purpose of influencing another person. You might flatter a person about their appearance, hoping that they'll accept your invitation to dinner. Or you might flatter your boss's management ability, hoping that she'll promote you or give you a raise. Flattery is always a bit exaggerated and always calculated for some ulterior purpose.

Compliments are honest, often spontaneous, and always free of charge. You compliment a coworker on his performance because you're honestly impressed. You compliment your spouse on their appearance because it is pleasing to you. You praise a child's growth or learning because you have a genuine desire to see them grow. A compliment must be sincere, and it must be offered without the hope of gaining something in return.

There is a saying that goes, "Show me a man who doesn't like praise, and I'll show you a man who doesn't like anything." Those who are liberal with compliments are natural influencers because people crave honest praise about themselves. People have a difficult time seeing themselves accurately, and positive feedback is always welcome. But most people do have enough self-awareness to spot flattery. They know when they're being played, and they come to resent it. Those who give honest compliments are sought out and valued.

Be generous with complimenting others. It costs you nothing to observe the best in another person. And it gains trust, furthers relationships, and builds influence.

Constructive Advice

Constructive advice is feedback or instruction given for the purpose of helping another person change, learn, or succeed. While some call this constructive criticism, I prefer the more positive term *advice* because the word *criticism* has come to have an entirely negative connotation.

Constructive advice is easy to formulate but challenging to deliver well. Other people's gaps in learning or ability are always easy to see, so it's often very easy to understand where they need to grow. However, people are naturally defensive about themselves and their shortcomings, so advice in any form is often unwelcome. Here are some things to remember when giving constructive advice.

First, the receiver must be open to it. Avoid offering unsolicited advice, no matter how noble your motivation may be. Wait for the person to ask for your opinion, or gently offer to share your expertise. If there is no permission to share your advice, it will be unwelcome and likely undermine your ability to influence the person further.

Second, hearing about your failing, shortcoming, or need for improvement is always difficult. Be gentle and always point your advice in a positive direction. I like to use the "sandwich method," placing constructive advice between two compliments. Here's an example: "Wow, I'm really impressed by how well you prepared for that presentation. Great job! Here is one idea that might help you deliver the material with greater impact. Again, I'm so impressed by the depth of information you shared." Hearing what they've done right always makes people more receptive to hearing how they could improve. And you can use this method in any setting, including with spouses, children, or neighbors.

Third, check your motivation. If your true desire is to vent irritation about a person's failings rather than to help them grow as a person, don't attempt to offer constructive advice. This is about the other person's growth and learning, not your frustration. Be sure that you're motivated by a genuine concern for others.

When done properly, constructive advice is a powerful form of positive speech. When you focus on others with the intention of helping them, it builds trust, respect, and influence.

Vision Casting

Vision casting is sharing your picture of the future with others in a way that inspires them to join you in creating it. This goes beyond making positive observations or finding the silver lining in a frustrating situation. It is defining a clear, positive vision for the future that excites the imagination of others and unlocks their motivation.

Many people confuse vision casting with goal setting, but the two are entirely different. Goals are specific, measurable, and time bound. They tell you exactly what you want to do next, and, in most contexts, you simply have to announce them, gain agreement, and then follow up to ensure they're achieved. "Paint the deck railing by the end of this month" is an example of a goal concerning home improvement.

Vision is different. It is a picture of an outcome, not a specific roadmap to achieving it. While a goal is a flat description of an achievement, a vision is an inspiring picture of the future. A vision for home improvement might be "to create an inviting, comfortable space for our family and friends."

Also, a goal can be created, posted, and reviewed occasionally to ensure progress. A vision must dwell within the mind, inspiring motivation nearly every day. A goal may be reviewed monthly or quarterly. A vision must be repeated over and over again until it becomes hardwired into one's thinking. So vision casting must be done continually, especially in casual situations.

Goals are announced at the annual meeting. Vision is reinforced in casual conversation. Goals are placed on a spreadsheet. Vision becomes part of your email signature. Goals often engender a sense of responsibility. Vision creates possibility.

When you repeat your vision frequently, positively, and hopefully, you inspire others to join you in making it reality. In that sense, vision casting is the foundational form of influence. It is the positive speech that most directly affects the thoughts and actions of others.

Truth Telling

Truth telling is being honest in any given situation. It is the perfect blend of tact and candor, saying what is true in a helpful manner that neither conceals, withholds, nor harms others. It is the opposite of spinning, which presents a distorted or self-centered view of reality.

Providing correct information is an important part of truth telling, obviously. But as we saw with the discussion on spinning, it is possible to use or omit factual information in a way that misleads others. Honesty goes beyond factual accuracy to give a true presentation of reality. When you have 17,421 subscribers to your blog, you could spin that number by saying that you have "some 20,000 daily readers." Or you could, more truthfully, say that "about 17,000 people receive my posts by email." If you are twenty minutes late for an appointment, you could, perhaps accurately, state that you got held up by an accident on the highway. Or, knowing that the accident caused only a ten-minute delay, you might more honestly say, "I'm sorry I kept you waiting."

It's important to remember, however, that being honest is not a license for being rude. Some people confuse the two, dishing out truthful but insensitive comments with the disclaimer, "I'm just the sort of person who speaks their mind," or, "I tell the truth and I don't care if you don't like it." Truth and tact are not mutually exclusive. While candid confrontation is sometimes necessary, it is nearly always possible to be honest and kind at the same time.

Here is the simple truth that those who get caught in the spin zone seem to forget: People find complete honesty refreshing, and they respect those who practice it. An ancient proverb holds that "an honest answer is like a kiss on the lips."[3] How true that is. In a world too often characterized by dishonesty and manipulation, it is pleasing to find an honest soul. That's why truthful people are always influential. When people realize that you are more committed to telling the truth than to protecting your ego or your agenda, they will trust and respect you all the more.

Apology

An apology is an admission of truth regarding your own failure, combined with a willingness to make amends. It is one of the rarest forms of positive speech because it requires deep humility. An apology requires a voluntary exposure of one's fault and places oneself at the mercy of another. It is risky and threatening, which is why so many people avoid apologizing.

As alternatives to apology, we often resort to defensive tactics such as ignoring, rationalizing, or blaming. We may pretend that we've done nothing wrong or that no breach in a relationship has occurred. "Problem? What problem?" we say, refusing to acknowledge what had happened. Or we may invent reasons why our behavior was necessary or why we are not truly at fault. We say things like, "It's not my fault; I was really tired," or "How was I supposed to know the project was due yesterday?" Worse, we may blame others, even the person we've wronged. We may throw around accusations such as, "She started it," or "If you had been on time none of this would have happened." Such tactics only make the situation worse. They deepen the rift in our relationship with others and undermine our influence.

To apologize is simply to admit the truth and offer to make amends. "I'm sorry I said that. I was in the wrong, and I'd like to make it up to you." "I didn't see the car parked there, and that was careless of me. I'm sorry about that, and I'm going to notify my insurance company right away."

When you are at fault in any situation, you gain respect and credibility by admitting the truth. Apart from being the right thing to do, which it always is when in the wrong, apologizing builds your influence over others because they come to see that you are truthful, even about yourself.

Start the Cycle

If you still doubt the power of positive words, consider this letter, which appeared some years ago in an advice column in the *Chicago Tribune*.

> In August of 1991, I was told I had brain cancer and my chances of living another five years were at best 50-50. When word of this leaked to my friends, two of them began a letter- and card-writing campaign. All the pilots employed by our airline got involved.
>
> The response was overwhelming. I received stacks of cards and letters every day. The doctors and nurses also let me know they were interested in my recovery and gave me a lot of T.L.C. The all-female team in the radiation department where I took my treatment deserves special mention

for its perpetual smiles and supportive attitude. My pilot buddies collected enough money to send me and my family to Disney World for a beautiful vacation.

Surrounded by all that love, I couldn't help but get better. I am now classified as a cancer survivor, and the support of my friends continues to this day. I am convinced that "friend therapy" can be a big factor in recovery.

To all those incredible people who helped me in my time of need, I say thank you and may God bless you.

Robert Berry, Shreveport, La.

Columnist Ann Landers responded: "While I am not suggesting that positive thinking can cure cancer, there is a great deal of evidence that the immune system does respond to what goes on in the brain. Thanks for a real upper. I'm sure you've spread a lot of joy today."[4]

Your words can have a dramatic, positive effect on those around you. Though your encouragement may not have the power to cure cancer, it will speed and support the recovery of those afflicted. Your words cannot singlehandedly transform the entire internet, but your gentleness and honesty can be a beacon of hope for those mired in manipulation and negativity. Your words cannot change reality, but they can inspire those around you to change it for themselves.

Positive thoughts beget positive words. And your positive words can reframe a negative situation, encourage a dispirited person, and point to a positive future. Your words do indeed have power. Use them well.

Notes

Chapter 1: The Power of a Positive Mind

1. Barbara L. Fredrickson, "The Broaden-and-Build Theory of Positive Emotions," *The Royal Society*, August 17, 2004, 1367, https://www.ncbi.nlm.nih.gov/pmc/articles/PMC1693418/pdf/15347528.pdf.

2. Ibid.

3. Ibid., 1375.

4. Napoleon Hill and W. Clement Stone, *Success Through a Positive Mental Attitude* (New York: Simon & Schuster, 1977), 81.

5. Stephen R. Covey, *The 7 Habits of Highly Effective People: Restoring the Character Ethic* (New York: Simon & Schuster, 1989), xxix.

Chapter 2: The Power of Optimism

1. Gottfried Wilhelm Leibniz, *Theodicy: Essays on the Goodness of God, the Freedom of Man and the Origin of Evil*, trans. E.M. Huggard (New York: Cosimo Books, 2009), 128.

2. This quote is popularly attributed to George Bernard Shaw, but the source of the quote itself is unknown.

3. Robert H. Schuller, *Move Ahead with Possibility Thinking* (New York: Jove Books, 1978), 15.

4. Robert F. Kennedy, "Remarks at the University of Kansas, March 18, 1968," website of the John F. Kennedy Presidential Library and Museum, https://www.jfklibrary .org/Research/Research-Aids/Ready-Reference/RFK-Speeches/Remarks-of-Robert -F-Kennedy-at-the-University-of-Kansas-March-18-1968.aspx.

Chapter 3: The Power of Modeling Mentorship

1. "Michigan 14-Year-Old Completes 40-Mile Trek While Carrying Brother on Back," *Fox News*, June 9, 2014, http://www.foxnews.com/us/2014/06/09/michigan-14-year-old-completes-40-mile-trek-while-carrying-brother-on-back/.

2. Jack Stahl, *Lessons on Leadership: The 7 Fundamental Management Skills for Leaders at All Levels* (New York: Kaplan Publishing, 2007), 64.

3. George Hathaway, *Leadership Secrets from the Executive Office* (New York: MJF Books, 2004), 13.

4. Ron McClung, "Positive Perspective," January 31, 2014, https://www.facebook.com/wesleyanpublishinghouse/posts/696983547020500.

5. Source unknown.

6. Shandra Martinez, "Rich DeVos: Family Assembly Created to Teach Grandchildren About Wealth," *MLive.com*, April 6, 2014, http://www.mlive.com/business/west-michigan/index.ssf/2014/04/rich_devos_family_assembly_cre.html#incart_river_default.

7. Hathaway, *Leadership Secrets from the Executive Office*, v.

8. Josh Bersin, "Spending on Corporate Training Soars: Employee Capabilities Now a Priority," *Forbes*, February 4, 2014, http://www.forbes.com/sites/joshbersin/2014/02/04/the-recovery-arrives-corporate-training-spend-skyrockets/.

9. Dave Ramsey, "7 Life Lessons from Truett Cathy," *DaveRamsey.com*, no date, http://www.daveramsey.com/blog/7-life-lessons-from-truett-cathy.

10. Stan Toler, *ReThink Your Life* (Indianapolis: Wesleyan Publishing House, 2008), 34.

Chapter 4: The Power of a Mission-Led Vision

1. Stan Toler, *Stan Toler's Practical Guide to Leading Staff: How to Empower Your Team and Multiply Ministry* (Indianapolis: Wesleyan Publishing House, 2012), 53.

2. John Swartz, "Michael Dell Beat Icahn, Now He's Reinventing PC Stalwart," *USA Today*, June 9, 2014, http://www.usatoday.com/story/tech/2014/06/09/michael-dell-rare-interview-pc-consolidation-battle-with-carl-icahn/9914017/.

3. Paul Argenti and Janis Forman, *The Power of Corporate Communications: Crafting the Voice and Image of Your Business* (New York: McGraw-Hill, 2002), 71.

4. David L. McKenna, *The Leader's Legacy* (Newberg, OR: Barclay Press, 2006), 21.

5. Max De Pree, quoted in Goodreads.com, http://www.goodreads.com/author/quotes/831.Max_DePree.

6. Margot Starbuck, "Women Leading in a New Era," *Christianity Today*, December 19, 2013, https://www.christianitytoday.com/women-leaders/2013/december/women-leading-in-new-era.html.

7. Pat Williams, *Coach Wooden: The 7 Principles That Shaped His Life and Will Change Yours* (Grand Rapids, MI: Revell, 2011), 79.

8. Nelson Mandela, quoted in Goodreads.com, http://www.goodreads.com/quotes/829582-what-counts-inlife-is-not-the-mere-fact-that.

9. John C. Maxwell, *The Right to Lead: Learning Leadership Through Character* (Nashville: Thomas Nelson, 2010), 41.

10. Jim Collins and Morten T. Hansen, *Great by Choice* (New York: Harper Business, 2011), 182.

11. Quoted in Toler, *Stan Toler's Practical Guide to Leading Staff*, 44.

12. Nicole Fallon, "14 Leaders Share Best Leadership Advice," *Business News Daily*, November 30, 2013, http://www.businessnewsdaily.com/5541-best-leadership -advice.html.

13. Mary Jo Asmus, "5 Ways to Notice Hidden Leadership Talent," Aspire Collaborative Services, June 25, 2014, http://www.aspire-cs.com/5-ways-to-notice-hidden -leadership-talent.

14. "Needs Assessment," http://en.wikipedia.org/wiki/Needs_assessment.

15. Mark A. Smith and Larry M. Lindsay, *Leading Change in Your World* (Newton, MA: Triangle Publishing, 2001), 160-61.

16. Kevin Cope, *Seeing the Big Picture: Business Acumen to Build Your Credibility, Career, and Company* (Austin, TX: Greenleaf Book Group Press, 2012), 93.

17. Jack Stahl, *Lessons on Leadership: The 7 Fundamental Management Skills for Leaders at All Levels* (New York: Kaplan Publishing, 2007), 10-11.

18. "Corporate Purpose," https://www.chick-fil-a.com/About/Who-We-Are.

19. Chuck Salter, "Chick-fil-A's Recipe for Customer Service," https://www.mosaicclubs .com/wp-content/blogs.dir/4635/files/sites/4635/2016/10/Chick-fil-As-Recipe-for -Customer-Service-_-Fast-Company-_-business-innovation.pdf.

20. Quoted in *Scrapbook.com*, http://www.scrapbook.com/quotes/doc/5065.html.

21. Kerry Hannon, "Sheryl Sandberg's 5 Best 'Lean In' Tips for Women," *Forbes*, March 13, 2013, http://www.forbes.com/sites/nextavenue/2013/03/13/ sheryl-sandbergs-5-best-lean-in-tips-for-women/.

22. Argenti and Forman, *The Power of Corporate Communication*, 74.

23. Jeffrey L. Cruikshank, *The Apple Way: 12 Management Lessons from the World's Most Innovative Company* (New York: McGraw Hill, 2006), 176.

24. Fallon, "14 Leaders Share Best Leadership Advice."

25. Georgea Kovanis, "Millennials Shape the New Holiday Shopping Experience," *Detroit Free Press*, November 23, 2014, http://www.freep.com/story/life/shopping/ georgea-kovanis/2014/11/23/millennials-shape-new-holiday-shopping-experience /19414121/.

26. McKenna, *The Leader's Legacy*, 61.

27. Ibid., 72.

Chapter 5: The Power of Courage in Challenging Times

1. Michael Hyatt, "The Top-10 Characteristics of Lousy Leaders," MichaelHyatt.com, September 1, 2014, https://michaelhyatt.com/lousy-leaders/.

2. W. Clement Stone quoted in Stan Toler, *ReThink Your Life* (Indianapolis: Wesleyan Publishing House, 2008), 118.

3. Peter Hirsch, *Success by Design: Ten Biblical Secrets to Help You Achieve Your God-Given Potential* (Minneapolis: Bethany House, 2002), 78.

4. Ibid., 108.

5. Nicole Fallon, "Four Common Leadership Mistakes (And How to Avoid Them)," *Business News Daily*, September 25, 2013, http://www.businessnewsdaily.com/5174 -avoiding-leadership-mistakes.html.

Chapter 6: The Power of Motivation

1. Meghan M. Biro, "Leadership Is About Emotion," *Forbes*, December 15, 2013, http://www.forbes.com/sites/meghanbiro/2013/12/15/leadership-is-about-emotion/.

Chapter 7: The Power of Personal Encouragement

1. Abigail Van Buren, "Exercise in Self-Esteem Is Lesson for a Lifetime," *Uexpress*, January 10, 1999, http://www.uexpress.com/dearabby/1999/1/10/exercise-in-self-esteem -is-lesson.

2. Garson O'Toole, "Be Kind; Everyone You Meet Is Fighting a Hard Battle," *Quote Investigator*, http://quoteinvestigator.com/2010/06/29/be-kind/.

3. Dale Carnegie, *How to Win Friends and Influence People*, rev. ed. (New York: Gallery Books, 1936), 227.

4. Ann Landers, "Simple Words Can Comfort," *SunSentinel*, December 30, 1993, http://articles.sun-sentinel.com/1993-12-30/lifestyle/9312290209_1_dear-ann -landers-new-jersey-woman-daughter.

Chapter 8: The Power to Transform

1. "Transformational Leadership," http://en.wikipedia.org/wiki/ Transformational_leadership.

2. Pearl Zhu, "Three 'T's' in Transformational Leaders," *Future of CIO*, http://future ofcio.blogspot.fr/2012/12/three-ts-in-transformational-leaders.html.

3. Janet Lee Reeder, "Transformational Leadership and Its Impact on Job Satisfaction and Employee Outcomes," unpublished manuscript, Saint Joseph's College of Maine.

4. Zhu, "Three 'T's' in Transformational Leaders."

5. Rich DeVos, *Ten Powerful Phrases for Positive People* (New York: Center Street, 2008), 88, 92.

6. Harvard Mental Health Letter, "In Praise of Gratitude," Harvard Health Publishing, November 2011, http://www.health.harvard.edu/newsletters/ harvard_mental_health_letter/2011/november/in-praise-of-gratitude.

7. DeVos, *Ten Powerful Phrases for Positive People,* 73.

8. Stan Toler and Robert Redwine, *Minute Motivators for the Military* (Kansas City, MO: Beacon Hill Press, 2014), 47.

9. David Allen, *Making It All Work* (New York: Penguin Group, 2008), 37.

10. Stan Toler, *Outstanding Leadership* (Eugene, OR: Harvest House, 2016), 141.

Chapter 9: The Power of Excellence

1. *What It Takes to Be Number One* ("derivative Work"), by Vince Lombardi and Vince Lombardi Jr, Simple Truths (2006, first edition), portions taken from the original Work, *What It Takes to Be #1, Vince Lombardi on Leadership*, McGraw-Hill Education, (2003), by Vince Lombardi Jr. Used with permission.

2. *Create a Life You Can't Wait to Live* ("derivative Work"), by Zig Ziglar, Simple Truths (2012), portions taken from the original Work, *Better Than Good*, Thomas Nelson, Inc. (2006), by Zig Ziglar. Used with permission.

3. George Bush, *Leadership: A Treasury of Great Quotations for Everybody Who Aspires to Be a Leader*, eds. William Safire, Leonard Safir (New York: Simon & Schuster, 1990), 22.

Chapter 10: The Power of a Positive Message

1. *The Power of Words*, "Our Story," Purplefeather, 2010, http://purplefeather.co.uk/our-story.

2. See Matthew 7:3-5.

3. Proverbs 24:26.

4. Ann Landers, "Surrounded by Love, He Was Ready for a Miracle," *Chicago Tribune*, March 2, 1993, http://articles.chicagotribune.com/1993-03-02/features/9303186542_1_dear-ann-landers-diets-don-t-work-long-distance-truck-driver.

Other Harvest House Books by Stan Toler

The Power of Your Attitude

As much as you try, sometimes you just can't change your circumstances—and never the actions of others. But you do have the power to choose how your attitude affects your outlook on your day and those you influence in your life.

Join Stan Toler as he shares the *what, why,* and *how* behind the transformation you desire. With this book, you'll...

- release the thoughts and habits that keep you from experiencing joy on a daily basis

- learn the seven choices you can make to get out of a rut and into greater success
- implement a plan to improve your outlook in three vital areas and conquer negativity

Having lost his father in an industrial accident as a boy, Toler knows about coping with unexpected tragedies and harsh realities. He will gently guide you through the internal processes that can positively change any life—including yours.

The Power of Your Brain

Do you find yourself stuck in negative thought patterns? Is your thinking disrupting your day and thwarting your goals?

When you choose to take each thought captive to the obedience of Christ, you drive out the world's way of thinking that breeds depression, discontent, and despair—and make room for more joy, faith, and purpose. Let bestselling author Stan Toler teach you an easy four-step process for restoring order to your brain:

- *Detoxification*—remove the clutter from your mind
- *Realignment*—establish your thoughts on God's truth
- *Reinforcement*—bring others along on the journey
- *Perseverance*—maintain your positive momentum

Take control of your thinking and embrace a new start—experience the freedom of a mind transformed by God!

Outstanding Leadership

What makes a leader stand out? What are the keys to truly making a difference? And how can you become the influencer you were created to be? With more than forty years of leadership experience, Stan Toler knows what it takes to empower people to reach organizational and personal goals. He cuts through the mystery and confusion and provides clear guidelines to help you accomplish vital leadership tasks, including...

- defining your vision, developing your plan, and communicating clearly to help people buy in to your shared goal
- overcoming common leadership challenges to create a culture of success
- building strong relationships and effective teams that make working hard worthwhile

You'll find all the tools, tips, and practical guidance you need to help individuals and groups reach their highest potential and fulfill their God-given purpose.

Minute Motivators for Leaders

You are a leader—people look to you to be an example, offer direction, and provide inspiration. But with so much to do, how can you keep fresh, focused, and excited about your opportunity to make a difference in people's lives? Stan Toler provides inspirational quotes, one-page gems of wisdom, and memorable taglines to fuel your passion and clarify your vision. You'll find plenty of helpful reminders that...

- leaders are in the people business. As a leader, your primary function is not to buy, sell, or ply a trade. It is to understand and work with people.
- bureaucrats run institutions. Leaders lead people. You can make the difference.
- leadership is a team sport. Do more than direct individuals—build a team.

This treasure of tried-and-true principles will be your on-the-go source for the motivation and encouragement you need to be the effective leader you were created to be.

Minute Motivators for Women
STAN TOLER AND LINDA TOLER

Whether you pick up this book first thing in the morning or when you're winding down at bedtime, you'll be inspired and encouraged over and over again! Author Stan Toler and his wife, Linda, share thought-provoking quotes and beautiful words of hope within these pages. Each chapter will draw your attention to a single attribute every godly woman wants to cultivate in her life, such as patience, wisdom, persistence, courage, and gratitude. Bite-size portions of inspiration make this the perfect devotional for, well, anytime—especially those days when you feel like you can never get ahead. Recharge in the middle of a hectic schedule or end your day with a much-needed reminder that God has every aspect of your life under control.

About the Author

Stan Toler (1950–2017) was a dynamic international speaker, having spoken in more than eighty countries of the world. He wrote over one hundred books, including his bestsellers *Minute Motivators for Leaders, The Secret Blend, The Relational Leader,* and *The Exceptional Leader.* His books have sold over three million copies.

For many years, Toler served as vice president and taught seminars for John C. Maxwell's INJOY Leadership Institute, training church and corporate leaders to make a difference in the world.

Toler Leadership
P. O. Box 720230
Oklahoma City, OK 73172-0230
Web: www.stantoler.com

To learn more about Harvest House books and
to read sample chapters, visit our website:

www.harvesthousepublishers.com

HARVEST HOUSE PUBLISHERS
EUGENE, OREGON